Five-Minute Gratitude

By

Jody Ortiz

ISBN- 978-1-96249012-2

Dedication

I dedicate this book to my daughter.

Your strength and courage amaze me every day. You've faced more than most ever will, yet you continue to meet life with grace, humor, and an unshakable light that inspires everyone who knows you. You've taught me that gratitude isn't just found in ease, it's born in endurance, in victories, and in the choice to keep believing in goodness even when life feels heavy.

You're the reason I still look for beauty in difficult places. Your resilience reminds me daily that hope can grow anywhere, and that love, once planted, never stops blooming.

"Choose people who lift you up."

Michelle Obama

Table of Contents

Just five minutes can change your day.

Introduction

FIVE MINUTES THAT CHANGED EVERYTHING

A few years ago, I picked up a book that promised to change my outlook on life through the simple act of gratitude. It encouraged readers to write ten things every day for which they were thankful.

Ten blessings.

Ten moments.

Ten reasons to appreciate life.

At first, I dove in eagerly, ready to transform my attitude and see my world through a new lens. Each morning, I sat with my notebook and pen, determined to fill every line with gratitude. But after a few days, something shifted. Instead of feeling inspired, I felt drained. I wasn't ungrateful. I was simply overwhelmed.

Some mornings, I couldn't think of ten things. I had only one or two that truly mattered, and yet I kept pushing myself to reach that number. I glanced around the room and searched for inspiration just to finish the list.

By day four, my gratitude journal looked like this:

1. Thank you for my daughter who is sweet and talented.

2. Thank you for my health because I enjoy the life I want.

3. Thank you for the drying rack that helps me keep up with the laundry.

4. I am so grateful for my jewelry that is so beautiful and precious.

5. I am blessed to have my bird, who has been companion.

6. Thank you for my closet that holds all of my clothes.

7. I am so grateful for my pasta maker that provides fresh pasta for the family.

8. I am blessed to have this bed that is so comfortable.

9. I am grateful for my sewing machine that helps me make clothes.

10. I am blessed to have a shower that gets me clean.

It was fine... but it didn't *move* me. My lists were thoughtful but hollow, mechanical rather than meaningful. By day twenty-four, I stopped explaining *why* I was thankful altogether:

1. Thank you for my family.

2. Thank you for my friends.

3. Thank you for all of the good things that are in my life.

4. Thank you for the birds.

5. Thank you for the moon.

6. Thank you for the stars.

I went through the motions, but I lost the heart behind the habit.

Still, I couldn't deny how much the book changed me. It made me more aware, more present, more conscious of the everyday miracles that often go unnoticed. But it also made me realize something deeper: gratitude doesn't thrive under pressure. It blossoms in simplicity.

When I finished the book, I found myself missing the daily practice but not the structure. The author encouraged readers to start again from the beginning, yet I wanted something new, something sustainable. I wanted to keep my heart open without feeling like gratitude was another task on my to-do list.

Gratitude came and went like a passing season.

That was the turning point for me. I realized I didn't need a long list to feel thankful. I just needed a moment. Five quiet minutes to reflect on one or two blessings that truly touched my heart that day. Five minutes to connect with what matters most.

So, I searched for a resource that offered exactly that... something brief yet powerful, simple yet profound. But I couldn't find it. There were endless apps, websites, and elaborate journals, but none that matched what I needed: a tangible book I could hold, one that invited me to slow down and reflect without demanding perfection or time I didn't have.

That's when *The Five-Minute Gratitude* book was born.

It began as a small idea, an addition to my personal blog where I could share reflections and daily exercises with others who also longed for something simple and sincere. Over time, it grew into a project of the heart, a daily reminder that gratitude doesn't have to be grand to be life-changing.

Each page in this book is designed to help you pause, breathe, and refocus on the beauty already within your reach.

You don't need thirty minutes or ten items. You just need five minutes and an open heart.

So, I invite you to join me on this journey. Let's take five mindful minutes each day to thank God, the universe, Mother Nature, or whatever you recognize as your source of strength and wonder. And if you don't have a higher power, that's okay too. Gratitude itself can become your practice, your stillness, your connection to something greater than circumstance. Together, we'll learn to notice the good that surrounds us, the people who love us, and the quiet moments that sustain us.

Gratitude isn't about how much you list. It's about how deeply you feel.

And sometimes, five minutes is all it takes to change everything.

How to Use This Book

The book's intention is to be a gentle companion... a quiet invitation to pause, reflect, and reconnect with the parts of yourself that the noise of life often drowns out. In a world that measures worth by productivity, and that rewards speed over stillness, and opinion over understanding, it's easy to forget that peace is something you can create, not something for which you wait.

Each reflection in this book has been carefully chosen to nurture your inner life and to help you find meaning in your daily experiences and to remind you of the beauty that persists, even in hardship. Some entries will inspire contemplation. Others may bring up emotion, memory, or release. Each one is designed to ground you in gratitude and gently guide you back to yourself.

FIVE MINUTES THAT CAN TRANSFORM YOUR DAY

Five minutes might not sound like much, but it's long enough to shift your energy, renew your perspective, and change the course of your day. These pages are not meant to overwhelm you with lengthy exercises or lofty goals. Instead, they invite you to pause for just five minutes to breathe, to notice, and to remember.

You can use your kitchen timer, the timer on your stove, or an app on your phone...whatever timing method you prefer. Once you begin, commit fully to those five minutes. Let the world wait. You deserve this moment of quiet restoration.

Each exercise follows a rhythm of reflection, stillness, gratitude, and release. You'll find a short intro or story to give you context to the exercise and open your heart, followed by a practical meditation or reflection–whatever terminology fits best into your beliefs—and a few journal prompts for deeper thought. You can use this as a daily ritual, a weekly reset, or a tool for healing when life feels heavy.

If you miss a day, simply return when you can. This is not an exercise in perfection. It's a practice in gentleness with life, with others, and with yourself.

SETTING YOUR SPACE

Before you begin each exercise, take a moment to create a small space for reflection. It doesn't need to be elaborate. It can be a corner in your living room, or your bed, or your front porch. You can add a touch of ambiance with a candle, a cup of tea, or a soft blanket... whatever you require to transform even a busy room into a sanctuary.

Many people find it helpful to read a passage aloud or whisper the gratitude phrase at the end of each reflection. Hearing your own voice affirm peace or healing has power.

You might choose to play soft instrumental music, light incense, or simply sit in silence. The key is consistency. Not in routine, but in intention. When you signal to your mind and body that this is your time to slow down, everything responds.

WHAT YOU'LL FIND INSIDE

The book is divided into thematic phases. Each one a stage of personal growth:

Phase 1: Grounding and Awareness – Learning to slow down, breathe, and be here now.

Phase 2: Compassion and Connection – Deepening your relationships with yourself and others.

Phase 3: Growth and Inner Strength – Building resilience, courage, and faith in your own endurance.

Phase 4: Abundance and Perspective – Reclaiming your sense of direction, joy, and spiritual clarity.

Each phase builds upon the one before it, but you don't have to read them in order. Trust your intuition. Let your heart guide you to the topic you need most that day: *Stillness, Forgiveness, Balance, Healing, Perseverance,* or *Freedom.* You can do the exercises in order or just flip through to what calls to you.

You may notice that many reflections weave in wisdom from poets, philosophers, saints, and teachers. You'll learn from voices like Maya Angelou, Toni Morrison, Frida Kahlo, and Marianne Williamson. These quotes were chosen not only for their beauty, but for their truth. They echo the shared human journey toward meaning, compassion, and inner peace.

HOW TO REFLECT AND JOURNAL

After reading the reflection, take a few breaths before beginning the five-minute exercise. The guided exercises are short on purpose to remind you that mindfulness doesn't require a retreat or hours of quiet. It requires only your presence.

When you reach the *Optional Journal Reflection* section, if you choose to do it, write without judgment. Don't worry about grammar, structure, or sounding "insightful." This is not about performance. It's just for you and it's about honesty. Let your thoughts flow freely. Some days your words may be full of emotion. On other days, they may be just a sentence or two. Both are perfect.

If you find yourself stuck, return to your breath.

Remember, journaling is a conversation with your soul. Some answers come quickly. Others arrive slowly, like dawn breaking after a long night.

You might even write the date at the top of each page so you can look back later and see how far you've come. Often, healing and growth happen unnoticed. We don't realize we've changed until we revisit our own words and see that we have.

HOW TO USE THE GRATITUDE PHRASE

Each reflection ends with a short gratitude phrase, a simple sentence like *"Thank you for the strength to endure,"* or *"Thank you for the wisdom to rest."* These phrases are more than words. They are affirmations designed to shift your inner dialogue.

You can whisper them, write them, say them out loud, or hold them in your heart. Over time, you'll notice that gratitude becomes a natural response, even to challenges. You'll begin to see blessings in places that once only felt like burdens. That's when transformation happens... not when life gets easier, but when your vision becomes clearer.

A LIVING PRACTICE

This book isn't meant to be read once and set aside. It's meant to be lived with and revisited, written in, and marked with your thoughts, tears, and triumphs. Think of it as a living document of your healing and growth. I've included pages of lines after each exercise to write on, but if you enjoy writing and feel called to write more, use a companion journal for your thoughts.

Return to certain passages when you need them most such as *Forgiveness* after conflict, *Balance* during busy seasons, *Faith* during uncertainty. Let it evolve with you.

The more you use it, the more personal it will become. Over time, your copy of this book will carry your handwriting, your energy, and your journey and it will become a tangible reminder of your resilience and capacity for renewal.

WHAT TO EXPECT ALONG THE WAY

Some reflections may bring comfort, while others may stir memories or emotions you thought you left behind. That's part of the healing process. Growth often requires revisiting old wounds. Not to relive them, but to release them.

When this happens, pause and breathe. Be gentle with yourself. Healing is not linear. You may move forward, circle back, rest, and rise again. All of it counts.

If emotions surface that feel too heavy to face alone, reach out to a friend, therapist, or trusted guide. Healing doesn't mean isolating yourself. It means allowing support to meet you where you are.

THE POWER OF SMALL MOMENTS

This book was designed around the principle that transformation doesn't require sweeping change. It begins with small, consistent moments of awareness. The five minutes you take to breathe, reflect, or write are enough to begin shifting your inner landscape.

Each practice, no matter how small, is an act of self-respect. Every time you turn to these pages, you're saying, *My peace matters. My healing matters. My life matters.*

And that simple act — the decision to show up for yourself — is how change begins.

WHAT YOU'LL RECEIVE

If you take only one thing from this book, let it be this: healing and gratitude are not destinations. They are daily practices. They are choices you make again and again, no matter how imperfectly.

Use this book as your anchor when life feels uncertain and as your companion when joy fills your heart. Come to it as you are, whether weary or hopeful, doubtful or curious, and let it remind you that you are never too far from peace.

Five minutes at a time, you are coming home to yourself.

Phase 1: Grounding and Awareness

1. Focus

"I find hope in the darkest of days and focus in the brightest. I do not judge the universe." Dalai Lama

Today's practice is about focus, which is the ability to be fully present with one thought, one action, or one intention at a time. In a world full of noise, distraction, and demands, focus is a quiet superpower. It's what separates a scattered day from a productive one, and a restless mind from a peaceful heart.

But focus isn't just about productivity. It's about presence. And when you're present, even for just five minutes, you can access clarity, calm, and gratitude.

An ancient story from the *Mahabharata* tells of a prince named Arjuna, one of the greatest archers of his time. His teacher, Dronacharya, placed a wooden bird in a tree and asked each student to aim at the bird's eye.

Before Arjuna's turn, the teacher asked others what they saw.

"I see the tree, the sky, and the bird," said one. "I see the bird and its wings," said another.

When Arjuna stepped forward, the teacher asked, "What do you see?"

"I see only the eye of the bird," Arjuna replied.

Dronacharya smiled and told him to release the arrow. It struck the eye perfectly.

Now, let's focus.

Using your kitchen timer, the timer on your stove, or an app on your phone, set your timer for five minutes.

Sit comfortably. Close your eyes and choose one thing to focus on... an area of your life you want to improve, a relationship that matters, a goal you've been avoiding, or even the simple act of breathing.

If you struggle with staying focused, let that be your focus today.

Take a deep breath and picture yourself completing your daily tasks one at a time, fully present.

Hold that vision. Let your breath slow. Stay with it. When the timer ends, say quietly, *"Thank you,"* for whatever you focused on.

Throughout the day, when your mind wanders, gently return to this morning's intention. Each time you do, say again, *"Thank you."*

Optional Journaling Exercise

Take a few quiet minutes to reflect on today's theme – Focus.

Ask yourself:

- What areas of my life need more of my attention right now?

- What distractions most often pull me away from what truly matters?

- How would my life feel if I gave up my full focus to the people, dreams, or habits that bring me joy?

- What small step can I take today to bring more mindful focus into my day?

Write freely without judgment. Let your thoughts flow naturally. When you're finished, close your journal, take a deep breath, and say, *"Thank you for my ability to focus."*

_____

_____

_____

_____

_____

_____

_____

_____

_____

_____

2. Home

"Home is the nicest word there is."
Laura Ingalls Wilder

A home is more than a house created from manmade materials; it's a place where you rest your body, relax, recharge, and feel safe and loved.

There are millions of people in the world who dream of having a home.

If you have walls around you and a roof over your head, you already have more than some.

It doesn't matter if your home is a multi-million-dollar estate or a small, rented apartment.

It doesn't matter what people say about your home. What matters is how it makes you feel.

Give thanks for your home.

Using your kitchen timer, the timer on your stove, or an app on your phone, set your timer for five minutes.

Close your eyes and picture yourself walking through the front door of your home.

Take a deep breath and let your senses come alive.

Breathe in the smells, the love, and the life you've built there.

Walk a little farther inside and look for the beauty and the fond memories.

Feel the love.

24

Say Thank You.

Keep that vision in your mind until the timer goes off, then open your eyes and say *Thank You* again.

As you go through your day, if you have negative thoughts about your home, replace them with gratitude and appreciation for what you have. Once you deeply feel and express gratitude for the home you have, you'll begin to attract something even grander.

Optional Journaling Exercise

Take a few quiet minutes to reflect on today's theme – Home.

Ask yourself:

- What is your favorite spot in your home, and why does it bring you comfort?

- When was the last time you felt completely at peace in your home?

- What memories fill your home with warmth or laughter?

- How can you show gratitude today for the space that shelters and supports you?

Write freely without judgment. Let your thoughts flow naturally. When you're finished, close your journal, take a deep breath, and say, *"Thank you for my home."*

3. Love

"A loving heart is the beginning of all knowledge." Thomas Carlyle

Every living creature desires love at some point on life's path.

It can vary from a deep, loyal friendship to a passionate affair.

It can come from a pet, a grandparent, a parent, a spouse, a sibling, a child, a grandchild, or a friend.

Where it comes from doesn't matter.

What matters is that we *feel* love for another living being and that we receive it in return.

Love is one of life's most powerful forces. It can lift you so high that you forget your worries, or it can pull you into the depths of despair. It brings both light and shadow, joy and sorrow, and it isn't always easy to balance.

A single word, glance, or gesture can change everything, turning a good day into a bad one, or an ordinary moment into something extraordinary.

Today, your focus is on setting an *intention* to let go of the negative and welcome more positive energy into your relationships.

Using your kitchen timer, the timer on your stove, or an app on your phone, set your timer for five minutes. Close your eyes and focus on the relationship that means the most to you. It could be a romantic partner, a beloved pet, a friend, or a family member.

With your eyes closed, travel back to a moment when you felt pure, undeniable love.

Was it the day you brought your pet home?

Your first kiss?

The first time you held your child?

The moment you realized someone had become your best friend?

Let that memory fill your heart.

Feel the warmth, the safety, and the joy.

Smile.

Say Thank You.

When you feel gratitude for the love already present in your life, you invite more of it in.

Love grows where gratitude lives.

Stay within that memory until the timer goes off. Then, take a deep breath, open your eyes, and say *Thank You* once more.

Throughout the day, carry that image within your heart. Each time you think of or see that person—or that cherished animal—return to that place of love.

True happiness is contagious, and when you feel it, you share it with the world.

Optional Journaling Exercise

Take a few quiet minutes to reflect on today's theme – Love.

Ask yourself:

- Who in your life makes you feel most loved, and how do they express that love?

- How can you show appreciation for the people or animals who bring you joy?

- When was the last time you allowed yourself to *truly* feel loved without fear or hesitation?

- What does unconditional love look like to you, and how can you nurture more of it in your life?

Write freely without judgment. Let your thoughts flow naturally. When you're finished, close your journal, take a deep breath, and say, *"Thank you for the love in my life."*

_____

_____

_____

_____

_____

_____

4. *Possibilities*

"Gratitude turns what we have into enough." Aesop

For those who wake each morning and only see what's missing, imagine those who live surrounded by lack and yet still choose to wake up to possibilities.

Whenever something feels absent from your life, that absence can easily become your focus.

You notice what others have, feel envy creeping in, and find yourself stuck in a constant loop of *wanting.*

When your focus is on what you lack, you unintentionally close yourself off to blessings.

Your energy remains tied to what's missing, instead of opening your heart to what's possible.

Today, you'll shift that focus.

You'll appreciate your blessings, even in areas that feel incomplete.

Desire is not wrong. It drives growth and creativity. But gratitude is what transforms desire into manifestation. To invite more good things into your life, be thankful for what you already have.

Using your kitchen timer, the timer on your stove, or an app on your phone, set your timer for five minutes.

Close your eyes and bring to mind one area of your life you wish could change.

What is your greatest desire?

It might be connected to your appearance, your finances, your home, or even a personal trait.

Now, instead of focusing on what you *don't* have, shift your thoughts to appreciation.

Don't say, "I don't like this," or "I wish it were different." Instead, say, "I am blessed to have this," and mean it.

For example:

"I am blessed to have a clothesline that helps me dry my clothes. Thank you for that clothesline."

"I am blessed to have hips that accentuate my waistline. Thank you for my hips."

Allow gratitude to fill the space where longing once lived.

Hold that vision until the timer goes off.

Take a deep breath, smile softly, and say *Thank You.*

Throughout the day, when your thoughts drift back to what you feel you lack, whisper *Thank You* again for the possibilities.

Gratitude turns absence into abundance.

Optional Journaling Exercise

Take a few quiet minutes to reflect on today's theme – Possibilities.

Ask yourself:

• What area of your life do you most often see through the lens of lack?

• How can you reframe that same area today through the lens of *possibility*?

• What simple blessing in your life do you often overlook?

• What might become possible if you chose to feel grateful right now, just as things are?

Write freely without judgment. Let your thoughts flow naturally. When you're finished, close your journal, take a deep breath, and say, *"Thank you for the possibilities in my future."*

_____

_____

_____

_____

_____

_____

_____

_____

5. Courage

"Children are happy because they don't have a file in their minds called 'All the things that could go wrong.'"
Marianne Williamson

Courage is something that comes naturally to children. They'll climb onto a roof, skate down a steep hill, dive headfirst into a pool, or sing and dance in front of strangers without hesitation.

They don't worry about the consequences or the embarrassment if something goes wrong.

They, as Nike says, "just do it."

They leap over and over off the backs of sofas, into pools, and into life itself. Every leap builds confidence. Every tumble teaches resilience.

If we could think more like a child, meaning unfiltered, daring, and curious, we might find that courage waiting within us.

Courage to start the conversation.

Courage to pursue the dream.

Courage to leap.

Using your kitchen timer, the timer on your stove, or an app on your phone, set your timer for five minutes. Close your eyes and place yourself in that fearless state you once knew as a child.

Think of at least one task you've been putting off because of fear.

It might be asking someone out, starting a side hustle, writing that book, learning an instrument, or signing up for a class.

What have you put off because of fear?

Now, in your mind, thank yourself for the courage you already have.

Say, *"Thank you for my courage."*

With your eyes still closed, envision yourself accomplishing that task and succeeding.

How does it feel?

How does your life change once you've done it?

Hold that feeling until the timer goes off. Take a deep breath and say again, *"Thank you for my courage."*

Throughout the day, whenever doubt or fear rises, repeat those words:

Thank you for my courage.

You are a warrior.

Own it.

Now, what are you waiting for?

Optional Journaling Exercise

Take a few quiet minutes to reflect on today's theme – Courage.

Ask yourself:

- What have you been avoiding out of fear, and why?

- How would your life improve if you found the courage to act?

- When was the last time you took a leap and surprised yourself with the result?

- What does being courageous mean to you in your daily life?

Write freely without judgment. Let your thoughts flow naturally. When you're finished, close your journal, take a deep breath, and say, *"Thank you for giving me courage."*

_____

_____

_____

_____

_____

_____

_____

_____

_____

6. *Hope*

"You may say I'm a dreamer, but I'm not the only one. Someday I hope you'll join us. And the world will live as one."

John Lennon

Gratitude and hope are closely linked in energetic vibration.

Gratitude looks at the here and now.

Hope looks at tomorrow.

Hope is what keeps you moving forward when the world feels dark or unforgiving.

It fills you up and lifts you high above your worries, carrying you on a soft cloud across the sky and giving you a reason to keep going.

Hope is your tomorrow... your promise that light always follows the storm.

Using your kitchen timer, the timer on your stove, or an app on your smartphone, set your timer for five minutes. Close your eyes and imagine yourself floating on a cloud made of hope.

Let it carry you gently through the sky.

Imagine your tomorrow... how it will look, feel, and unfold.

Give thanks for today.

Then give thanks for tomorrow.

Picture yourself smiling, heart light and full, feeling that spark of renewal that hope brings.

Hold that feeling. Let it fill you until the timer goes off.

Take a deep breath and whisper, *"Thank You."*

As you move through your day, if something negative or worrisome arises, reach for that cloud of hope and let it lift you again.

Like Annie famously said, "The sun will come out tomorrow."

And it will because you carry its light within you.

Optional Journaling Exercise

Take a few quiet minutes to reflect on today's theme – Hope.

Ask yourself:

- What does hope look like to you right now, in this season of your life?

- When was the last time you felt true, unwavering hope about your future?

- What are you most hopeful for, and how can gratitude today help bring it closer?

- How does hope change the way you view your challenges?

44

Write freely without judgment. Let your thoughts flow naturally. When you're finished, close your journal, take a deep breath, and say, *"Thank you for giving me hope."*

_____

_____

_____

_____

_____

_____

_____

_____

_____

_____

_____

_____

_____

7. *Peace*

*"Gratitude makes sense of your past,
brings peace for today, and creates a
vision for tomorrow." Unknown*

Starting your day by giving thanks for what you have grounds you.

It centers your thoughts and shapes the temperament you'll carry as life unfolds.

Gratitude creates a thoughtful mindset... one that helps you respond to others with love, patience, and grace. A daily gratitude practice cultivates peace within you, a peace you carry throughout your day and quietly pass on to others.

Peace doesn't mean the absence of noise or struggle; it means a heart that stays calm in the midst of both.

Using your kitchen timer, the timer on your stove, or an app on your phone, set your timer for five minutes. Close your eyes and picture what peace means to you.

Perhaps it's a quiet morning with a warm cup of coffee or tea on a sunlit porch or watching birds flutter through the trees. Maybe it's standing atop a mountain, looking down upon an endless blanket of green. Or it could be the feeling of sand beneath your feet as gentle waves roll in and wash away your worries.

Go to that peaceful place in your mind. Give thanks for the memories you've made in those places or the ones you've yet to create.

Stay there until the timer goes off, then open your eyes and softly say, *"Thank You."*

As you move through your day, return to that peaceful place whenever you feel anxious or hurried.

Let the calmness you cultivated within your meditation guide you back to balance and gratitude.

And, as we say in the Catholic Church, *"Peace be with you."*

Optional Journaling Exercise

Take a few quiet minutes to reflect on today's theme – Peace.

Ask yourself:

- What does true peace feel like to you physically, emotionally, and spiritually?

- When was the last time you experienced a deep sense of peace?

- What small changes could you make today to invite more peace into your daily life?

- How can you extend the peace you feel within yourself to others around you?

Write freely without judgment. Let your thoughts flow naturally. When you're finished, close your journal, take a deep breath, and say, *"Thank you for giving me peace."*

8. *Patience*

"Have patience with all things, but first of all with yourself." Saint Francis de Sales

In the 14th-century poem titled *Piers Plowman* by English poet William Langland, the famous line "Patience is a virtue, of which little is found in man" was made immortal.

Whether Langland was the first to say it or he merely preserved an older truth, his words still ring through the centuries. Patience is one of humanity's quietest strengths. It's virtue that asks us to slow down, to trust, and to release control.

When creating miracles or inviting positive change into your life, patience is essential. Growth doesn't happen in a single breath; it unfolds in its own divine rhythm. Gratitude grounds you in the present moment, and patience helps you carry that peace into what comes next.

Using your kitchen timer, the timer on your stove, or an app on your phone, set your timer for five minutes. Close your eyes and imagine what your life would feel like if patience guided every moment.

Picture yourself breathing easily, your heart unhurried, your mind free of worry or tension.

See yourself handling life's interruptions with calm understanding, and meeting others and yourself with grace.

Stay in that space until the timer goes off. Then open your eyes, take a slow breath, and softly say, *"Thank You."*

As you move through your day, return to that inner place of patience whenever frustration or restlessness appears. Patience doesn't remove obstacles. It teaches you to walk through them with peace.

Optional Journaling Exercise

Take a few quiet minutes to reflect on today's theme – Patience.

Ask yourself:

- In what area of your life do you most need to practice patience right now?

- How does impatience affect your thoughts or emotions?

- What would it feel like to trust that things will unfold in their own time?

- How can patience help you nurture gratitude in your daily life?

Write freely without judgment. Let your thoughts flow naturally. When you're finished, close your journal, take a deep breath, and say, *"Thank you for giving me patience."*

9. Stillness

*"In the midst of movement and chaos,
keep stillness inside of you."
Deepak Chopra*

Today is all about stillness.

We often rush through our days, our thoughts tumbling over each other like waves in a storm. But stillness is not the absence of movement. It's the presence of peace. It's the pause between breaths, the quiet space where clarity is born.

One morning, I caught myself moving from task to task without really being *there*. The coffee was cold on the counter, my phone buzzed with another reminder, and my thoughts were already three steps ahead.

So I stopped.

I stepped outside and into a world still wrapped in early light. The air was cool and heavy with dew, the only sound a distant bird calling from somewhere unseen. I took a slow breath and felt the quiet settle over me like a soft blanket.

For a moment, everything stilled. I didn't hear the noise. I didn't feel the worry. Even the rush inside my mind went quiet. I realized that stillness isn't something you find *out there*; it's something you uncover *within*. It's the space between breaths, the gentle awareness that life continues even when you stop chasing it.

For the next five minutes, give yourself permission to stop. Using your kitchen timer, the timer on your stove, or an app on your phone, set your timer for five minutes.

Close your eyes and imagine what your life would feel like if you found the stillness within yourself.

Sit comfortably and take a slow, deep breath in as you feel your lungs expand and your shoulders relax.

Exhale gently, releasing tension with the air that leaves your body.

Let your thoughts drift by like clouds in the sky, noticed, but not chased. If a worry rises, thank it for visiting, then let it float away. If a memory appears, smile at it, then allow it to fade.

After your timer ends, open your eyes and whisper softly: *"Thank you for the calm within me."*

Optional Journaling Exercise

Take a few quiet minutes to reflect on today's theme – Stillness.

Ask yourself:

- When do I feel most at peace?

- What distractions keep me from finding stillness?

- How does my body feel when I allow myself to pause?

- What simple things bring me calm. Are they sights, sounds, or sensations?

Write freely without judgment. Let your thoughts flow naturally. When you're finished, close your journal, take a deep breath, and say, *"Thank you for creating stillness within me."*

_____

_____

_____

_____

_____

_____

_____

_____

_____

_____

_____

_____

_____

_____

_____

10. Breath

"Inhale the future, exhale the past."
Unknown

In Tai Chi, there is a mindful movement where you gather all the negative energy within you and then release it through your breath. With slow, intentional motion, you draw in what feels heavy or stagnant, guide it down to your center, and then lift it toward your heart before exhaling it out. This flow is both physical and spiritual. It's a way of cleansing the body and restoring balance.

In today's gratitude practice, you'll do a similar movement, using your breath as a tool for release and renewal. The goal is to keep only the breath that serves you — the calm, the peace, the gratitude — and let everything else go.

Using your kitchen timer, the timer on your stove, or an app on your phone, set your timer for five minutes. Close your eyes and focus on your breathing.

With your palms facing upward and fingertips touching, rest your hands in your lap.

As you **inhale**, slowly raise your hands up your body, gathering everything that feels negative or burdensome from your core to your chest.

When your hands reach your heart, **turn your palms outward** and **exhale**, gently pushing that energy away from your body.

Repeat this flow — inhaling to gather, exhaling to release — until the timer ends.

When you finish, open your eyes and softly say, *"Thank you for the breath that sustains me."*

Optional Journaling Exercise

Take a few quiet minutes to reflect on today's theme – Breath.

Ask yourself:

- What emotions or thoughts surfaced as you focused on your breath?

- What did it feel like to release what no longer serves you?

- How does your body feel now compared to when you began?

- What are three things your breath helps you do — physically, emotionally, or spiritually — that you're grateful for today?

Write freely without judgment. Let your thoughts flow naturally. When you're finished, close your journal, take a deep breath, and say, *"Thank you for my breath."*

_____

_____

_____

11. Presence

*"Do not dwell in the past, do not dream of
the future, concentrate the mind on the
present moment."* Buddha

The electronic age in which we live has quietly taken away our ability to be fully present. Wherever you go — to a doctor's office, waiting for take-out, sitting in a movie theater before showtime, or even at a live event — most people around you aren't truly *there*. Their eyes are fixed on glowing screens instead of the world before them.

Life continues to move, yet we miss so much of it. Moments with loved ones slip by unnoticed. Conversations fade before they begin. We're losing our ability to connect on a deeper human level because we've replaced eye contact with emojis and real dialogue with typed words that often lose tone, warmth, and meaning.

We're living, but we're not present.

Today's exercise will help you return to that space of true awareness and connection.

Using your kitchen timer, the timer on your stove, or an app on your phone, set your timer for five minutes.

Close your eyes and recall the last time you were *fully present* with another human being. What was that moment like? Did you share laughter, conversation, or simple silence? If it was a stranger, did you discover something in common?

Stay in that memory. Observe how it feels to be fully engaged, to listen, to notice, and to connect.

Were you curious about them, or did you let the moment pass too quickly?

Breathe deeply, stay there, and simply *be present in the presence.*

When the timer ends, open your eyes and say, *"Thank you for allowing me to be present."*

Optional Journaling Exercise

Take a few quiet minutes to reflect on today's theme – Presence.

Ask yourself:

- What does being fully present mean to me in this season of my life?

- When do I find it hardest to stay in the moment, and what usually pulls me away?

- What small, everyday moments make me feel most alive and aware?

- How can I bring more mindfulness and gratitude into ordinary tasks like breathing, walking, or listening?

Write freely without judgment. Let your thoughts flow naturally. When you're finished, close your journal, take a deep breath, and say, *"Thank you. I am present."*

12. Simplicity

"Simplicity is the ultimate sophistication."
Leonardo da Vinci

When life is simple, it creates space to focus on what truly matters.

On fashion design shows like *Project Runway*, mentors often remind designers that simplicity can be powerful, as long as the details are executed with care. You don't need all the bells, whistles, or extra fluff. Too much clutter—whether in your home, your design, or your mind—dulls creativity and distracts from what's essential.

Keeping life simple opens the door for imagination and inspiration to flow freely.

Using your kitchen timer, the timer on your stove, or an app on your phone, set your timer for five minutes.

Close your eyes and let go of every thought cluttering your mind. Bring your attention to your heart and ask yourself: *what truly needs my focus today?*

Is it your marriage, your child, your parent, a friend, an acquaintance, a beloved pet, a project, or simply your peace?

Choose one thing and stay there. Breathe deeply and let everything else fade away until the timer ends.

When the timer ends, open your eyes and say, *"Thank you for giving me simplicity."*

Optional Journaling Exercise

Take a few quiet minutes to reflect on today's theme – Simplicity.

Ask yourself:

- What areas of my life feel cluttered or complicated right now, and how might I simplify them?

- When was the last time simplicity brought me peace or clarity?

- What would my day look like if I approached it with simplicity at its center?

- How can I remind myself that simplicity doesn't mean lack; it means focus and freedom?

Write freely without judgment. Let your thoughts flow naturally. When you're finished, close your journal, take a deep breath, and simply say, *"Thank you."*

_____

_____

_____

_____

_____

_____

13. *Reflection*

"Without deep reflection, one knows from daily life that one exists for other people."
Albert Einstein

Reflection is the art of looking inward to understand how we connect outward.

It reminds us that our actions, words, and even our silence ripple through the lives of others. In the rush of daily life, it's easy to forget that we are all threads in the same tapestry; our presence woven into someone else's story.

I watch a lot of reality television, and it's fascinating to see how cast members change from season to season after watching themselves through someone else's lens. They're forced to confront how their behavior—whether kind or cruel, loud or quiet—affects everyone around them. The experience often brings out both their best and their worst.

Deep reflection, much like what those reality stars face, invites you to pause and consider not just *who you are*, but *who you are to others*.

What kind of energy do you bring into a room? What emotions do you leave behind?

What small kindnesses—or sharp words—linger in the hearts of those around you?

What imprint do you leave on the memories of others?

Using your kitchen timer, the timer on your stove, or an app on your phone, set your timer for five minutes.

Close your eyes and take a slow, deep breath. Think of three people whose paths you've crossed today, or recently, if you're doing this exercise before interacting with others. Picture their faces. What did you bring into each interaction? Did you offer calm, compassion, patience, or joy?

If the answer is yes, smile and say thank you. If the answer is no, forgive yourself and imagine how you might bring a different energy next time. These exercises are not meant to make you feel bad about your actions, but to help you reflect, and to recognize what you've done well and where there's room to grow.

When the timer ends, open your eyes and say, *"I exist for others, and they for me."*

Optional Journaling Exercise

Take a few quiet minutes to reflect on today's theme – Reflection.

Ask yourself:

- How do I influence the emotions and energy of those around me?

- When was the last time someone's kindness or reflection changed my day?

- What does it mean to "exist for others" without losing myself?

- How can I make reflection a regular practice to strengthen my compassion and awareness?

Write freely without judgment. Let your thoughts flow naturally. When you're finished, close your journal, take a deep breath, and simply say, *"Thank you for giving me a moment to reflect."*

_____

_____

_____

_____

_____

_____

_____

_____

_____

_____

_____

_____

_____

14. Morning Light

*"Every morning we are born again. What
we do today is what matters most."*
Buddha

If moonlight is magical, then morning light is limitless. It carries the quiet promise that life, no matter how heavy yesterday felt, can begin again. The morning doesn't judge what came before. It simply offers its golden forgiveness. With each sunrise, the slate is wiped clean, giving us permission to start fresh.

Morning light softens the edges of regret and replaces darkness with possibility. It pours through the window, touching everything with warmth, whispering, *"You are still here. You still have time."*

Each dawn is an invitation to step forward with intention, to speak kindly, to move gently, and to try again.

In that first light, the world feels wide open and waiting. The past loosens its grip, and what lies ahead gleams with potential. Morning light is not just the beginning of a new day. It's a quiet reminder that we are endlessly capable of renewal and of creating a better today and a more hopeful tomorrow.

Using your kitchen timer, the timer on your stove, or an app on your phone, set your timer for five minutes.

Close your eyes and take a slow, deep breath. Think about what you want to do with this new day.

Do you want to create something new, begin a hobby you've been putting off, or step outside your comfort zone and do something completely unexpected?

Let the morning light fill your mind with possibility. Picture yourself moving through the day with purpose, curiosity, and gratitude for the simple gift of starting again.

When the timer ends, open your eyes and say, *"Thank you for the morning light and the chance to begin again."*

Optional Journaling Exercise

Take a few quiet minutes to reflect on today's theme – Morning Light.

Ask yourself:

- What does a fresh start mean to me today?

- What one small action could make today feel meaningful or new?

- How can I carry the energy of morning light throughout my day, even when challenges arise?

- What am I grateful to release from yesterday so I can move forward freely?

Write freely without judgment. Let your thoughts flow naturally. When you're finished, close your journal, take a deep breath, and simply say, *"Thank you for giving me another day."*

Phase 2: Connection and Compassion

15. Friendship

*"A friend is one who overlooks your
broken fence and admires the flowers in
your garden." Unknown*

Friendships keep you grounded and bring you joy. They draw you out of loneliness and give you purpose.

When life gets busy, when you're rushing from one commitment to the next, true friends remind you who you are, offer you a safe space, and reflect back what you sometimes forget. They don't just share your laughter. They catch you when you fall.

Research shows that our social connections—especially the quality and depth of our friendships—aren't just good for our hearts and minds: they also influence how long and how well we live. For example:

- A large meta-analysis found that across 148 studies with over 300,000 participants, people with stronger social relationships had a 50% greater likelihood of survival compared to people with weaker social ties.[1]

- In a recent longitudinal study of older adults in the U.S., stronger friendship networks (measured by size, contact frequency, and quality) were associated with reduced

---

[1] Social relationships and mortality risk: a meta-analytic review – https://pubmed.ncbi.nlm.nih.gov/20668659/

risk of all-cause mortality (about 24% lower risk) and reduced risk of stroke (about 19% lower risk).[2]

- In the region of Okinawa in Japan, where many people live past 100 years, one of the key features of community life is "moai" groups. These are long-standing social support groups among multi-generational friends who meet regularly, share meals, walk together, and support each other socially, emotionally and financially.[3]

These numbers help underline what friendship truly offers: a buffer against isolation, a provider of emotional resilience, and a contributor to physical health.

So when you think of your friends, think of them not just as fun companions or confidants, but as partners in your life's journey. Their presence can be as vital as the air you breathe, especially when life's storms hit.

Using your kitchen timer, the timer on your stove, or an app on your phone, set your timer for five minutes.

Close your eyes and take a slow, deep breath. Picture someone who brings light and value to your life.

A friend doesn't have to fit a traditional mold. It could be a parent, a sibling, a beloved pet, or even an online friend who makes you laugh when you need it most. Think of the one

---

[2] United we thrive: friendship and subsequent physical, behavioural and psychosocial health in older adults (an outcome-wide longitudinal approach) – https://pubmed.ncbi.nlm.nih.gov/37964589/

[3] Want to live a long, healthy life? 6 secrets from Japan's oldest people – https://www.weforum.org/stories/2021/09/japan-okinawa-secret-to-longevity-good-health/

(or few) who truly see you. Who do you confide in and trust? Who makes you smile, even on difficult days?

Focus on that friendship and fill your heart with gratitude. Imagine sending them warmth and positivity as if your energy could reach them across any distance.

Today, you're intentionally choosing to celebrate that bond and the joy it brings to your life.

When the timer ends, open your eyes and say, *"Thank you for my friend."*

Optional Journaling Exercise

Take a few quiet minutes to reflect on today's theme – Friendship.

Ask yourself:

- Who in my life makes me feel most understood, and why?

- What is one small way I can show appreciation for a friend today?

- How have my friendships shaped who I am becoming?

- In what ways can I be a better, more present friend to others?

Write freely without judgment. Let your thoughts flow naturally. When you're finished, close your journal, take a deep breath, and simply say, *"Thank you for giving me a friend."*

16. Family

*"Family isn't always blood. It's the people
in your life who want you in theirs; the
ones who accept you for who you are."
Unknown*

Family, whether bound by blood or found through lasting friendships, are the people who have seen both the good and the bad in our lives and choose to stay anyway. They're the ones who show up when the rest of the world grows quiet. Family is the truest form of unconditional love, the kind that doesn't demand perfection or performance, only presence.

Sometimes family is the one we're born into, and sometimes it's the one we build. It can be a parent, a sibling, a child, a lifelong friend, or even a chosen circle that becomes our safe haven. These are the people who remind us who we are when we forget, who anchor us when life feels uncertain, and who celebrate our small joys as if they were their own.

Family is where forgiveness lives, where laughter echoes through hard times, and where belonging takes root.

With this in mind, using your kitchen timer, the timer on your stove, or an app on your phone, set your timer for five minutes.

Close your eyes and take a slow, deep breath. Picture your family, the one you were born into or the one you pieced together and send them all the light and love that they have created within you.

Focus on your family and fill your heart with gratitude. Imagine sending them warmth and positivity as if your energy could reach them across any distance.

Picture a golden thread tying you to your chosen family and radiate love through that thread.

When the timer ends, open your eyes and say, *"Thank you for my family."*

Optional Journaling Exercise

Take a few quiet minutes to reflect on today's theme – Family.

Ask yourself:

- Who in my life feels most like family, and what makes that bond so meaningful?

- What is one way I can express gratitude to my family—by birth or by choice—today?

- How has my understanding of family changed as I've grown?

- What qualities do I most value in the people I consider family?

Write freely without judgment. Let your thoughts flow naturally. When you're finished, close your journal, take a deep breath, and simply say, *"Thank you for my family."*

17. *Kindness*

*"No act of kindness, no matter how small,
is ever wasted." Aesop*

Kindness is the quiet medicine the world forgets it needs. It costs nothing yet heals everything it touches. One kind word, one patient gesture, one moment of compassion can shift the energy of an entire day for you and for someone else.

We often underestimate the ripple effect of kindness. A smile exchanged with a stranger, a text checking in on a friend, or a soft word spoken instead of anger can transform a heavy moment into something lighter. Kindness requires no audience and asks for no reward; it's a gift that multiplies every time it's shared.

Science even supports what our hearts already know. Acts of kindness release serotonin and oxytocin, lowering stress and boosting feelings of connection. The more kindness we give, the more grounded and peaceful we become.

In a world often driven by division, kindness is both rebellion and remedy. It doesn't erase pain, but it soothes it. It doesn't solve every problem, but it reminds us that we're not alone in them.

"Kindness is the cure for all that divides, wounds, and weakens us. It's the quiet pulse that keeps humanity alive." — *Jody Ortiz*

Using your kitchen timer, the timer on your stove, or an app on your phone, set your timer for five minutes.

Close your eyes and take a slow, deep breath. Picture the faces of the people you've interacted with recently. Your family, friends, coworkers, or even strangers. Think of one person who might need kindness today.

As you breathe, imagine surrounding them with warmth, patience, and understanding. Let your heart fill with the intention to offer kindness, not for recognition, but simply because it's the most healing energy you can give.

When the timer ends, open your eyes and say, *"May kindness flow through me and into the world."*

Optional Journaling Exercise

Take a few quiet minutes to reflect on today's theme – Kindness.

Ask yourself:

- What simple act of kindness made a difference in my life recently?

- How does offering kindness change the way I feel about myself?

- Who in my life could use a kind word or gesture today?

- How can I make kindness my first response, even when it's difficult?

Write freely without judgment. Let your thoughts flow naturally. When you're finished, close your journal, take a deep breath, and simply say, *"Thank you for showing me kindness."*

18. Generosity

"No one has ever become poor by giving."
Anne Frank

Generosity is more than an act. It's a way of being. It's the quiet decision to share what you have, whether it's time, kindness, or a listening ear. In the Catholic Church, instead of tithing money, we tithe time, talent, or treasury, whatever we have to give.

True giving doesn't ask for anything in return. It simply recognizes abundance and passes it forward.

When we give freely, we shift our focus from what we lack to what we have. The smallest gesture, be it a smile, a compliment, or a moment of patience, can ripple outward in ways we'll never fully see.

Today, take five minutes to breathe gratitude for all that has been given to you, and all that you have the ability to give.

Using your kitchen timer, the timer on your stove, or an app on your phone, set your timer for five minutes.

Close your eyes and focus on a time when someone's generosity touched your life. Feel the warmth of that moment, the ease it brought, and the connection it created.

When your timer ends, open your eyes and say, *"Thank you for the generosity that flows to me and through me."*

Optional Journaling Exercise

Take a few quiet minutes to reflect on today's theme – Generosity.

Ask yourself:

- When have I felt most grateful for someone's generosity?

- What do I give freely that doesn't cost anything but means everything?

- How can I show generosity toward myself today?

- What might change in my relationships if I led with a more generous heart?

Write freely without judgment. Let your thoughts flow naturally. When you're finished, close your journal, take a deep breath, and simply say, *"Thank you for all the generosity I've been given."*

_____

_____

_____

_____

_____

_____

_____

_____

19. Empathy

"Empathy is a quality of character that can change the world." Barack Obama

There is an old story about a boy who was walking along the beach, tossing stranded starfish back into the ocean one by one.

A man approached him and said, "There are thousands of starfish on this shore. You'll never make a difference."

The boy bent down, picked up another starfish, and gently threw it back into the waves. "It made a difference to *that one,*" he said.

Empathy is what moves us to reach out to help others. Not because we can fix everything. But because we *feel* the pull of another's pain or joy and choose to act with love. It reminds us that every small gesture matters, and that kindness, even in quiet form, can ripple outward far beyond what we can see.

Today's practice is to pause and listen with your heart. When we let ourselves truly feel with others, not for them, but *with* them, we begin to heal both ourselves and the world around us.

Using your kitchen timer, the timer on your stove, or an app on your phone, set your timer for five minutes.

Close your eyes and think of someone who is struggling or hurting. As you breathe in, imagine sending them calm and comfort.

As you exhale, release any judgment or distance between you. Repeat this, filling the space between you with compassion.

When your timer ends, say, *"Thank you for the love that allows me to feel with others."*

Optional Journaling Exercise

Take a few quiet minutes to reflect on today's theme – Empathy.

Ask yourself:

- When was the last time someone truly listened to me with empathy? How did it make me feel?

- How do I show empathy in my daily life through words, actions, or silence?

- What keeps me from feeling empathy at times, and how can I gently remove that barrier?

- Who in my life could use my understanding and kindness today?

Write freely without judgment. Let your thoughts flow naturally. When you're finished, close your journal, take a deep breath, and say, *"Thank you for giving me the gift of empathy."*

_____

_____

_____

_____

20. Forgiveness

"It's one of the greatest gifts you can give yourself, to forgive. Forgive everybody."
Maya Angelou

As my mentor, Marianne Williamson once said, "Forgiveness is not always easy. At times it feels more painful than the wound we suffered, to forgive the one that inflicted it. And yet, there is no peace without forgiveness."

Forgiveness is not about excusing what happened. It's about freeing yourself from the weight of it. The human body carries emotional pain in physical ways. Stress, resentment, and unspoken anger can manifest as tension, fatigue, illness, or disease. When we hold on to bitterness, it doesn't harm the one who hurt us; it harms *us*.

Long ago in India, there lived a mighty emperor named Aśoka. He ruled with great power, but his hunger for conquest left fields of the fallen behind him. After one devastating battle, Aśoka walked among the dead. There were slain soldiers, villagers, and even children. The silence was deafening. The victory he chased felt hollow when he realized the immense suffering he caused.

In that moment, something within him broke open. The pain of others became his own, and he realized that the only true victory was over hatred itself. Asoka laid down his weapons and turned toward compassion. He spent the rest of his life spreading peace, planting trees, building hospitals, and teaching that forgiveness, of self and of others, is the root of healing.

From that day, he was no longer remembered for the wars he won, but for the peace he created. His story reminds us that even after great harm, forgiveness can transform not only a person, but a nation. In the current times we're facing, it's important to remember that peace will come.

As Asoka learned, forgiveness is a sacred act of self-love. It's the moment you decide to release the story that keeps you tied to pain and open the door to peace instead.

Using your kitchen timer, the timer on your stove, or an app on your phone, set your timer for five minutes.

Close your eyes and think of someone who causes you great emotional turmoil, someone whose actions hurt you.

Take a deep breath in, and as you exhale, imagine letting go of the cord that binds you to that pain.

Repeat softly in your mind: *"I release you, not because you deserve it, but because I deserve peace."*

When your timer ends, open your eyes and say, *"Thank you for the freedom forgiveness brings."*

Optional Journaling Exercise

Take a few quiet minutes to reflect on today's theme – Forgiveness.

Ask yourself:

- What does forgiveness mean to me right now, and what does it *not* mean?

- Who in my life do I still need to forgive, and what would releasing that pain feel like?

- Have I forgiven myself for mistakes or choices I still carry?

- How might my life change if I made forgiveness a daily practice?

Write freely without judgment. Let your thoughts flow naturally. When you're finished, close your journal, take a deep breath, and say, *"Thank you for giving me the strength to forgive."*

---

21. Understanding

"We don't see things as they are, we see them as we are." Anais Nin

Each of us views the world through the lens of our own experiences, education, and upbringing. What we see and how we interpret it are shaped by the stories that have formed us. This means that two people can look at the same situation and see something entirely different, and that's what makes human connection so beautiful.

Understanding doesn't require us to agree. It asks us to listen with curiosity instead of judgment. When we pause long enough to consider another perspective, we expand our own. In doing so, we soften our edges, deepen our compassion, and begin to see that every person is simply doing their best with the view they've been given.

True understanding transforms difference into discovery, and that is where empathy and peace begin.

There is an ancient story of six blind men who came upon an elephant for the first time. Each man touched a different part of the animal and tried to describe what he felt.

One touched the tusk and said, "An elephant is like a spear."

Another, touching the leg, said, "No, it's like a tree."

The third, holding the tail, insisted, "You're both wrong. It's like a rope."

They argued, each certain he was right. But none of them could see the full truth, only their part of it.

A wise traveler overheard them and said gently, "You are all correct, and you are all mistaken. Each of you holds one piece of the truth, but only together can you understand the whole."

Understanding doesn't come from being right. It comes from being willing to *see more.*

Using your kitchen timer, the timer on your stove, or an app on your phone, set your timer for five minutes.

Close your eyes and think of a moment when you disagreed with someone, a friend, family member, or even a stranger. Imagine looking through *their* eyes for a moment.

What might have shaped their view? What fears or hopes could have guided their words?

As you breathe in, picture yourself opening to a wider understanding. As you exhale, release the need to be right.

When your timer ends, say, *"Thank you for helping me see beyond my own view."*

Optional Journaling Exercise

Take a few quiet minutes to reflect on today's theme – Understanding.

Ask yourself:

- When was the last time I felt truly understood by someone? What made that possible?

- How does it feel when I listen with curiosity instead of trying to be right?

- Whose perspective in my life could I try to see more clearly today?

- What have my past experiences taught me about compassion and open-mindedness?

Write freely without judgment. Let your thoughts flow naturally. When you're finished, close your journal, take a deep breath, and say, *"Thank you for giving me the ability to see beyond my own viewpoint."*

_____

_____

_____

_____

_____

_____

_____

_____

_____

_____

22. Support

"We teach girls to shrink themselves, to make themselves smaller. But you can't truly support other women until you stop apologizing for your own power."
Chimamanda Ngozi Adichie

True support begins when we stop dimming our own light to make others comfortable. When a person embraces their strength, they give quiet permission for others to do the same. We're not in competition. We're reflections of what's possible when courage meets compassion.

To support another person is to say, *I see your brilliance, and it doesn't take away from mine.* It's standing shoulder to shoulder instead of toe to toe. It's knowing that their success does not diminish your worth. It amplifies it.

When people uplift one another, entire communities rise. The power of genuine support is contagious, healing, and revolutionary.

Using your kitchen timer, the timer on your stove, or an app on your phone, set your timer for five minutes.

Close your eyes and think of someone who has supported or inspired you. Someone who helped you find your voice, your courage, or your peace.

As you breathe in, feel gratitude for their presence in your life.

As you exhale, imagine sending strength and encouragement back to them.

If you can, reach out to them today and let them know how much they've meant to you.

When your timer ends, say, *"Thank you for those who lift me, and for the power within me to lift others."*

Optional Journaling Exercise

Take a few quiet minutes to reflect on today's theme – Support.

Ask yourself:

- Who are the people who have helped me grow, and how did their support change me?

- How can I celebrate another person's success without comparison or doubt?

- In what ways have I downplayed my own power, and how can I reclaim it?

- What does true mutual support look like to me?

Write freely without judgment. Let your thoughts flow naturally. When you're finished, close your journal, take a deep breath, and say, *"Thank you for giving me support in my life."*

_____

_____

_____

23. Trust

"Trust yourself. Think for yourself. Act for yourself. Speak for yourself. Be yourself."
Marva Collins

Trust begins within yourself. It's easy to look outward for validation by seeking reassurance in others' approval or agreement. But real trust — the kind that grounds you — grows from believing in your own voice, your intuition, and your ability to navigate uncertainty.

When you trust yourself, you stop asking for permission to exist as you are. You speak with more honesty, love more freely, live more authentically, and make choices that align with your truth instead of fear.

Self-trust isn't built overnight. It's strengthened each time you keep a promise to yourself, follow your instincts, or choose integrity over comfort. Every small moment of courage becomes another thread in the fabric of inner faith you weave.

When you learn to trust yourself, life opens. You stop controlling outcomes and start allowing them to unfold.

Using your kitchen timer, the timer on your stove, or an app on your phone, set your timer for five minutes.

Close your eyes and take three slow, deep breaths. Think about a time when you doubted yourself, but acted anyway, and it turned out well.

What guided you in that moment? What did it feel like to trust your own wisdom?

As you breathe in, silently say, *"I trust myself."*

As you exhale, release any need to prove your worth to anyone else.

When your timer ends, open your eyes and say, *"Thank you for the voice within me that knows the way."*

Optional Journaling Exercise

Take a few quiet minutes to reflect on today's theme – Trust.

Ask yourself:

- When have I relied on my intuition and been grateful I did?

- What makes it difficult for me to trust myself fully?

- How can I rebuild trust with myself after breaking a promise to me?

- What would my life look like if I truly believed in my own guidance?

Write freely without judgment. Let your thoughts flow naturally. When you're finished, close your journal, take a deep breath, and say, *"Thank you for my strength and ability to trust myself."*

24. Community

"We live in a world in which we need to share responsibility. It's easy to say, 'It's not my child, not my community, not my world, not my problem.' Then there are those who see the need and respond. I consider those people my heroes."
Mr. Fred Rogers

Growing up in the '70s and early '80s, I watched *Mister Rogers' Neighborhood* and *Captain Kangaroo* every chance I could. They were gentle voices of kindness in a world that didn't always value inclusivity. Mr. Rogers, especially, became my moral compass, my very own Jiminy Cricket. He showed me that being part of a community means noticing the needs of others and responding with compassion.

Community is built one small act of care at a time. It's saying hello to a neighbor, lending a hand without being asked, or choosing to listen instead of turning away. Every time we give of ourselves, we strengthen the invisible thread that connects us all.

We don't need to save the whole world. We just need to take responsibility for our part in it. That's where real community begins. Now, more than ever in my lifetime, community and our care and concern for each other makes a difference to those in need.

Using your kitchen timer, the timer on your stove, or an app on your phone, set your timer for five minutes.

Close your eyes and think of a moment when someone made you feel like you belonged. It could be a teacher, friend, neighbor, or even a stranger.

Breathe in gratitude for that person and the kindness they showed you.

As you exhale, imagine passing that same feeling forward to someone else today.

When your timer ends, say, *"Thank you for the people who remind me I am part of something greater."*

Optional Journaling Exercise

Take a few quiet minutes to reflect on today's theme – Community.

Ask yourself:

- Who in my life makes me feel most connected, supported, and seen?

- What small act can I do today to strengthen my community?

- When have I witnessed kindness that inspired me to do better?

- How does giving to others give back to me in unexpected ways?

Write freely without judgment. Let your thoughts flow naturally. When you're finished, close your journal, take a deep breath, and say, *"Thank you for my community."*

25. Companionship

*"Friendship is a single soul dwelling in
two bodies." Aristotle*

Companionship is one of life's purest gifts. It's the quiet understanding between two souls who don't need to explain themselves to be seen. True companionship isn't about constant presence. It's about *knowing* someone is there, even in silence.

To find a true companion is to discover a reflection of your own heart, someone who helps you see yourself more clearly, love more deeply, and laugh more freely. A companion can be a fellow human being, or a furry, scaled, or winged friend who listens without words and loves without condition.

Companionship isn't limited by form. It's defined by presence. Sometimes it's the friend who knows what you're feeling before you speak, or the animal who curls beside you when the world feels heavy. Companions meet us where words end in understanding, loyalty, and quiet joy.

They remind us that connection is a universal language. Whether shared through laughter, gentle eyes, or the brush of a paw or wing, companionship brings comfort in our loneliest moments and magnifies our happiness in our brightest ones.

When we nurture companionship — human or otherwise — we remind our hearts that love is not measured by how alike we are, but by how deeply we care.

Using your kitchen timer, the timer on your stove, or an app on your phone, set your timer for five minutes.

Close your eyes and think of a friend or companion who has stood beside you through the seasons of your life.

As you breathe in, remember the moments that strengthened your bond. Think of the laughter, the honesty, the shared silence.

As you exhale, send them silent gratitude and love. If you can, reach out later today to remind them how much they mean to you.

When your timer ends, say, *"Thank you for the souls who walk beside me."*

Optional Journaling Exercise

Take a few quiet minutes to reflect on today's theme – Companionship.

Ask yourself:

- Who has been a steady companion in my life, and what makes our bond strong?

- How do I show up as a companion to others when they need me most?

- What qualities do I value most in friendship?

- How has companionship helped me grow into a more compassionate version of myself?

Write freely without judgment. Let your thoughts flow naturally. When you're finished, close your journal, take a deep breath, and say, *"Thank you for my companions."*

26. Listening

"Listening is a revolutionary act."
Gloria Steinem

In a world filled with noise, listening has become rare and therefore radical. To truly listen is to give another person space to be seen and heard without interruption, without judgment, without tuning them out while thinking of your answer, and without rushing to respond. It's one of the purest forms of love we can offer.

Listening asks us to quiet the inner chatter that wants to fix, advise, or compare. It invites us instead to simply *be present* with another soul. When we listen deeply, we begin to understand not only others but also ourselves, our biases, our triggers, and our capacity for empathy.

Each act of listening builds connection. It reminds someone that their story matters. It teaches us that peace often begins, not with speaking louder, but with hearing better and paying attention to someone outside of ourselves.

Using your kitchen timer, the timer on your stove, or an app on your phone, set your timer for five minutes.

Close your eyes and take a slow, deep breath.

Think of the last conversation you had where you felt truly heard or when you listened with your full attention. What made that moment different? What did it feel like to be seen and understood?

As you breathe in, imagine filling your heart with openness.

As you exhale, release the need to respond... just listen.

When your timer ends, say, *"Thank you for the voices that teach me, and the silence that helps me hear."*

Optional Journaling Exercise

Take a few quiet minutes to reflect on today's theme – Listening.

Ask yourself:

- When was the last time I listened without interrupting or planning my reply?

- How does it feel when someone truly listens to me?

- What might I learn if I listened more and spoke less?

- How can I create more space in my life for quiet and understanding?

Write freely without judgment. Let your thoughts flow naturally. When you're finished, close your journal, take a deep breath, and say, *"Thank you for giving me the ability to listen."*

_____

_____

_____

_____

27. Harmony in Relationships

"Raise your words, not voice. It is rain that grows flowers, not thunder." Rumi

My paternal grandfather was a WWII POW veteran and a quiet man of few words. When he spoke, everyone listened. He didn't use his voice to scold or shame but to teach, uplift, and remind us of what truly mattered. His calm strength carried more weight than any loud opinion ever could.

It's remarkable how some people move through life softly yet leave an unshakable mark. Their harmony comes not from volume, but from presence... from knowing that wisdom doesn't need to shout to be heard.

True harmony in relationships comes when we listen more than we speak, when we choose compassion over correction, and when our words fall gently enough to help something grow.

Using your kitchen timer, the timer on your stove, or an app on your phone, set your timer for five minutes.

Close your eyes and think of someone whose calm or kindness has shaped you. Someone whose voice brought peace instead of noise.

As you breathe in, picture the sound of their steadiness guiding you.

As you exhale, imagine sending that same calm outward into your own relationships.

When your timer ends, say, *"Thank you for the voices that bring peace instead of thunder."*

Optional Journaling Exercise

Take a few quiet minutes to reflect on today's theme – Harmony in Relationships.

Ask yourself:

- Who in my life models harmony through gentle strength or thoughtful words?

- How do I communicate when I'm hurt or misunderstood, and how could I do so with more calm and care?

- What situations tempt me to raise my voice instead of my understanding?

- How might my relationships change if I responded with patience instead of reaction?

Write freely without judgment. Let your thoughts flow naturally. When you're finished, close your journal, take a deep breath, and say, *"Thank you for giving me a harmonious home."*

_____

_____

_____

_____

_____

28. Faith in Humanity

*"In spite of everything, I still believe that
people are really good at heart."*
Anne Frank

In my last confession, I told my priest that I was struggling not to judge others. With everything happening in the world — the rise in racism, greed, and division — and when Covid started, when so many refused to take simple steps to protect one another, I couldn't see the good in humanity anymore.

He sighed softly and said, "That's a tough one." He agreed that sometimes it's hard to see past all the bad to the good.

When I first converted to Catholicism in 1998, my priest at the time, Father Ken — who later passed away from cancer — told me something I've never forgotten. He said that when you die and go to Heaven, you might be asked just one question: *What did you do for your fellow man?*

That has guided my life ever since my confirmation. Every day, I try to consider how my actions affect others, how my choices ripple outward, and how I can do a little good in the lives of those around me. In doing so, I honor Father Ken's lesson and strive to keep my faith in humanity alive.

Using your kitchen timer, the timer on your stove, or an app on your phone, set your timer for five minutes.

134

Close your eyes and think of one person who has restored your faith in humanity, maybe through a kind act, a moment of honesty, or a selfless deed.

As you breathe in, picture their goodness like a small light.

As you exhale, imagine that light spreading through the world, one person at a time.

When your timer ends, say, "Thank you for reminding me that goodness still lives in the human heart."

Optional Journaling Exercise

Take a few quiet minutes to reflect on today's theme – Faith in Humanity.

Ask yourself:

- Who has inspired me to believe in goodness again when I was losing faith?

- How do I contribute to the good I wish to see in the world?

- What small, everyday acts remind me that people are capable of kindness?

- How can I honor those who've guided me toward compassion and hope?

Write freely without judgment. Let your thoughts flow naturally. When you're finished, close your journal, take a deep breath, and say, *"Thank you for restoring my faith in humanity."*

Phase 3: Growth and Inner Strength

29. Faith

"Faith is the evidence of things unseen. It is the belief that even in the darkest night, the stars still shine." Maya Angelou

Faith healers have existed in nearly every culture throughout history from ancient temples to village shrines, from desert nomads to mountain monks. While their methods may differ, one truth remains the same: their strength lies not in the ritual itself, but in the unwavering belief that healing is possible.

This isn't a call to abandon medicine or reason or the advice of your trusted doctor, but rather a reminder of how powerful faith can be in ourselves, in others, and in something greater than what we can see.

Science tells us that belief alone can influence the body. They have mapped out how the mind and spirit are intricately tied. Faith doesn't deny reality. It reshapes how we face it. Sometimes, when everything else has been stripped away, faith is what carries us through the storm.

One of my favorite stories on this topic comes from the city of Jerusalem at the time of Christ. There was a woman who had been ill from chronically bleeding and therefore deemed "unclean" for twelve years. Doctors gave up on her, and her strength was nearly gone. One day, she heard that a great teacher named Jesus was passing through the crowd. Weak and trembling, she pushed through the people, believing that if she could only touch the hem of his robe, she would be healed.

When her fingers brushed the fabric, she felt her pain lift. Jesus turned and said, "Daughter, your faith has saved you. Go in peace and be cured of your affliction." Mark 5:25–34

It wasn't his robe or the crowd or the moment that cured her. It was her belief that healing was still possible when all hope seemed lost. Her faith became her bridge from suffering to peace.

That same kind of faith lives within us. It's the faith that tomorrow can be brighter, that healing is possible, and that love can find its way through the cracks of even our hardest days.

Using your kitchen timer, the timer on your stove, or an app on your phone, set your timer for five minutes.

Close your eyes and think of a time when you had to trust without proof, when all you had was hope and the quiet whisper of faith.

As you breathe in, imagine light filling the unseen spaces of your heart.

As you exhale, release doubt and fear, letting your faith stand in their place.

When your timer ends, say, *"Thank you for the faith that sustains me when sight and certainty are gone."*

Optional Journaling Exercise

Take a few quiet minutes to reflect on today's theme – Faith.

Ask yourself:

- When has faith carried me through a time of uncertainty or fear?

- What does faith mean to me... in myself, in others, or in something greater?

- How can I nurture faith even when I don't feel it strongly?

- What does it look like to live as though I already trust that everything will work out for my highest good?

Write freely without judgment. Let your thoughts flow naturally. When you're finished, close your journal, take a deep breath, and say, *"Thank you for giving me faith."*

_____

_____

_____

_____

_____

_____

_____

_____

30. Resilience

*"Resilience is accepting your new reality,
even if it's less good than the one you had
before. You can fight it, you can do
nothing but scream about what you've
lost, or you can accept that and try to put
together something that's good."*
Elizabeth Edwards

Resilience is not about pretending that everything is fine. It's about learning to stand in the middle of the storm and still believe in your ability to find the sun again. It's the strength that rises quietly after loss, the courage that takes shape when the plan falls apart, and the grace that whispers, *I will begin again.*

Elizabeth Edwards knew something about that kind of strength. She faced heartbreak, public betrayal, and illness with honesty and hope. Her life reminds us that resilience doesn't mean returning to what once was. It means creating something meaningful from what remains.

Whenever I think of resilience, I think of my daughter. In 2016, she was diagnosed with multiple incurable and life-altering conditions — Reflexive Sympathetic Dystrophy, Postural Orthostatic Tachycardia Syndrome, Raynaud's, and Erythromelalgia. RSD or sometimes referred to as CRPS is so severe it's often called the most painful condition known to medicine. For nearly six years she could not walk or care for herself, yet she never gave up.

She found ways to heal where medicine had no answers through natural therapies in a machine that improves her circulation, by switching to a plant-based vegan diet, and through powerful mental exercises that help her manage pain and reclaim peace. Instead of sinking into what she lost, she built a new reality... one grounded in hope, strength, and purpose.

She's my living reminder that resilience is an act of faith — faith in yourself, in your purpose, and in the belief that even in brokenness, beauty can still be born.

Using your kitchen timer, the timer on your stove, or an app on your phone, set your timer for five minutes.

Close your eyes and take a deep breath.

Think of a moment when life changed in a way you didn't expect. When your path took a turn you hadn't planned. Feel the ache of that shift, but also the quiet strength that helped you survive it.

As you breathe in, say silently, *"I am still here."*

As you exhale, whisper, *"I am growing through this."*

When your timer ends, open your eyes and say, *"Thank you for the resilience that lives within me and the faith that keeps me standing, even when the wind howls."*

Optional Journaling Exercise

Take a few quiet minutes to reflect on today's theme – Resilience.

Ask yourself:

- What moment in my life most tested my strength, and what did I learn about myself through it?

- How do I know when I'm being resilient, even if I don't feel strong?

- What helps me rise when life feels heavy? Is it faith, love, purpose, or something else?

- How can I honor the parts of my story that shaped me without letting them define me?

Write freely without judgment. Let your thoughts flow naturally. When you're finished, close your journal, take a deep breath, and say, *"Thank you for making me resilient."*

_____

_____

_____

_____

_____

_____

_____

_____

_____

_____

31. Confidence

"Confidence cannot develop fully until mastery has been accomplished. But mastery itself is confidence born of love."
A Course in Miracles

Confidence isn't loud or showy. It's the quiet trust that who you are is enough. It's knowing that your worth isn't measured by perfection but by presence. True confidence doesn't come from control, appearance, or achievement; it comes from love. It's the steady kind that reminds you that you are already whole.

I spent nearly a year in a mentorship program led by Marianne Williamson, learning to become a miracle-minded coach. I had always been curious about *A Course in Miracles*, and I thought, *Who better to learn from than one of its greatest teachers?*

At the time, I was living in deep fear. Because of my work in true crime and advocacy for the wrongfully convicted. For several years, I was stalked and watched so closely that I rarely left my home. My world became small, shadowed by fear of what might happen next.

Then, a wise therapist reminded me that **fear is an illusion**. It's a barrier that blocks the flow of life. When the opportunity arose to study with Marianne, I jumped in with both feet. Through her guidance and the teachings of *A Course in Miracles*, I learned to see fear for what it is: the absence of love.

Slowly, confidence replaced my fear. I learned to trust myself again, to walk outside with my head high, and to believe that I was protected... not because life was suddenly safe, but because I remembered that love was stronger than fear.

A Course in Miracles teaches that confidence born of love is rooted in something eternal. When you know that divine love walks beside you, fear loses its grip. Confidence becomes less about proving and more about allowing — allowing yourself to be guided, supported, and strengthened by the truth that you are never alone.

Confidence is not arrogance; it's peace. It's walking forward with an open heart, even when you can't see the next step. It's trusting that the strength you need will be there when you arrive.

Using your kitchen timer, the timer on your stove, or an app on your phone, set your timer for five minutes.

Close your eyes and take a slow, deep breath in through your nose, and exhale gently through your mouth.

Think about an area of your life where fear has held you back, something you've hesitated to do, say, or become.

Now imagine divine love standing beside you, hand outstretched, reminding you that you are safe and capable. The divine love can be God, Buddha, a goddess, nature, or whatever you claim as your higher power.

As you breathe in, say, *"Love is my strength."* As you exhale, whisper, *"I release the fear that keeps me small."* Continue this rhythm until your timer ends, breathing in love and breathing out fear.

When you open your eyes, say, *"Thank you for the confidence that comes from knowing I am guided by love."*

Optional Journaling Exercise

Take a few quiet minutes to reflect on today's theme – Confidence.

Ask yourself:

- What fears have I outgrown, and what helped me move through them?

- How does love show up as confidence in my daily life?

- When have I trusted my inner guidance, even when I couldn't see the outcome?

- How can I practice confidence born of love rather than ego or control?

Write freely without judgment. Let your thoughts flow naturally. When you're finished, close your journal, take a deep breath, and say, *"Thank you for giving me confidence."*

_____

_____

_____

_____

_____

_____

_____

32. Authenticity

*"Hard times arouse an instinctive desire
for authenticity." Coco Chanel*

Authenticity often reveals itself in our hardest seasons. When life tests us, the masks fall away, and what remains is truth... who we really are beneath expectation, performance, and fear. Hardship has a way of clarifying what matters. It strips us down to the essentials: integrity, courage, and heart.

To live authentically is to stop seeking approval and start honoring alignment. To act, speak, and love in ways that match our soul's rhythm. It's a return to wholeness, a quiet coming home.

When we stand in authenticity, we invite others to do the same. Our honesty becomes a mirror that reflects permission, reminding those around us that vulnerability and strength can exist side by side.

Coco Chanel understood what it meant to rebuild from nothing. Born into poverty and raised in an orphanage after her mother's death, she learned early that survival demanded strength and truth. When life stripped away comfort and certainty, she discovered the beauty of simplicity and the power of being unapologetically herself.

Her hardships didn't harden her. They clarified her. From those humble beginnings, she created a timeless legacy rooted in elegance and independence. Chanel changed the world of fashion not by following others, but by daring to express who she truly was. Her story reminds us that authenticity is not born in ease. It's shaped in resilience.

When we live in authenticity, we not only free ourselves, we give others permission to do the same.

Using your kitchen timer, the timer on your stove, or an app on your phone, set your timer for five minutes.

Close your eyes and think of a time when hardship revealed something real about you. A truth you hid away or forgot.

As you breathe in, remember the strength that truth gave to you.

As you exhale, release the need to be anything other than who you are.

When your timer ends, say, "Thank you for the freedom that comes from being real."

Optional Journaling Exercise

Take a few quiet minutes to reflect on today's theme – Authenticity.

Ask yourself:

- When have life's challenges revealed my truest self?

- What parts of me feel most authentic and what parts still wear armor?

- How can I bring more honesty and courage into my daily life?

- Who in my life inspires me to live more freely and truthfully?

Write freely without judgment. Let your thoughts flow naturally. When you're finished, close your journal, take a deep breath, and say, *"Thank you for allowing me to be unapologetically me."*

_____

_____

_____

_____

_____

_____

_____

_____

_____

_____

_____

_____

33. Determination

"Fight for the things that you care about,
but do it in a way that will lead others to
join you." Ruth Bader Ginsburg

Determination doesn't always roar. Sometimes it's the steady persistence of showing up again and again, even when progress feels slow or unseen. Ruth Bader Ginsburg embodied that kind of grace in motion. Her quiet resolve shaped history, not through anger, but through purpose and patience.

She taught us that determination guided by compassion can change the world. True strength isn't in winning every battle. It's in fighting for what matters most while keeping your dignity intact. Determination is holding your ground with kindness, your vision with clarity, and your heart with courage.

Every act of perseverance plants a seed of change, of justice, and of hope. When we act with integrity and intention, our determination becomes contagious, drawing others toward the same light.

Using your kitchen timer, the timer on your stove, or an app on your phone, set your timer for five minutes.

Close your eyes and think about something you deeply care about... something that stirs your heart and won't let go.

As you breathe in, feel your resolve strengthen.

As you exhale, imagine releasing the doubt that tells you it's too hard or too late.

Let determination settle into your spirit like a calm fire. Feel it as steady, unwavering, and pure.

When your timer ends, say, *"Thank you for the strength to keep going, and for the grace to lead with love."*

Optional Journaling Exercise

Take a few quiet minutes to reflect on today's theme – Determination.

Ask yourself:

- What is something I believe in so strongly that I'm willing to keep showing up for it?

- How can I pursue my goals with both passion and patience?

- Who has modeled determination for me in a way that inspired grace rather than aggression?

- How can I lead by example so others feel empowered to join me in what I care about most?

Write freely without judgment. Let your thoughts flow naturally. When you're finished, close your journal, take a deep breath, and say, *"Thank you for giving me the strength, patience, and determination to reach my goals."*

34. *Balance*

*"We need to do a better job of putting
ourselves higher on our own 'to-do' lists."
Michelle Obama*

Balance is not about doing everything. It's about knowing what deserves your energy. We often pour ourselves into others, such as our families, our work, and our responsibilities until there's nothing left to give. Balance reminds us that caring for ourselves is not selfish; it's essential.

Michelle Obama's words echo a truth many women forget: you cannot pour from an empty cup. When you take time to nourish your body, mind, and spirit, you strengthen the foundation on which everything else rests. Balance isn't found in perfection. It's found in alignment, in listening to what your soul needs, and responding with kindness.

When life pulls in every direction, pause. Breathe. Ask yourself what truly matters in this moment. Sometimes the most productive thing you can do is rest.

For years, I worked as a ghostwriter and editor, writing and editing over a hundred books, plus articles and online publications for others. I also transcribed interviews, volunteered for the St. Vincent de Paul Society, taught CCD — the Catholic version of Sunday school — homeschooled my daughter, and even drove for Meals on Wheels.

At the same time, I was living with several health conditions, including Sjögren's syndrome. As a trained bookkeeper who mostly worked in accounting jobs, I was advised to file for social security because I might never work again. But I thought, *my brain still works. I can write.* And I did. Once my business began to thrive, I didn't know how to turn it off. I worked until my eyelid muscles gave out from exhaustion. Literally. That was my diagnosis.

Eventually, I learned that balance doesn't come from pushing harder. It comes from learning when to stop. I had to put myself and my family first, to remember that peace is not something you earn. It's something you choose.

Using your kitchen timer, the timer on your stove, or an app on your phone, set your timer for five minutes.

Close your eyes and take a slow, deep breath.

Picture yourself as a vessel... strong but finite. Each time you give, you pour a little of yourself out. Now imagine refilling that vessel with light, peace, and energy as you breathe in.

As you exhale, release guilt, obligation, and the pressure to do it all.

As you inhale, whisper softly, *"I am enough."*

Let stillness remind you that your worth isn't measured by your productivity, but by your presence.

When your timer ends, say, *"Thank you for the wisdom to rest when I am weary and to fill my own cup with grace."*

Optional Journaling Exercise

Take a few quiet minutes to reflect on today's theme – Balance.

Ask yourself:

- What does balance look like for me right now? Not in theory, but in daily life?

- When do I notice myself running on empty, and what helps me replenish?

- How can I protect my energy without feeling guilty for saying no?

- What would change if I treated rest as a sacred part of productivity, not the opposite of it?

Write freely without judgment. Let your thoughts flow naturally. When you're finished, close your journal, take a deep breath, and say, *"Thank you for giving me balance."*

_____

_____

_____

_____

_____

_____

_____

_____

35. Acceptance

"If you don't like something, change it. If you can't change it, change your attitude." Maya Angelou

Acceptance doesn't mean giving up. It means finding peace where struggle no longer serves you. It's the moment when you stop fighting against what is and start working with it. Life doesn't always give us the power to control our circumstances, but we always have the power to choose how we respond to them.

Maya Angelou's words remind us that acceptance and empowerment are intertwined. When we can't change what's around us, we can change what's within us. The shift from resistance to grace is where growth begins.

A Course in Miracles teaches a similar truth in Lesson 10: *"My thoughts do not mean anything."* It teaches that our suffering often comes not from what happens, but from the stories we tell ourselves about what happens. When we attach meaning, judgment, or fear to an event, we give it power over us. Acceptance begins when we pause and remember that our thoughts are not facts. They are simply passing clouds in a vast, calm sky.

This lesson invites us to release our mental grip on how things *should* be. It reminds us that peace doesn't come from controlling our world, but from quieting the mind that insists it knows best. When we stop assigning blame or expecting perfection, we can finally see reality with compassion.

Acceptance is not passive; it's a gentle form of strength. It's looking at a challenge and saying, *"This too belongs to my story."*

Acceptance invites us to meet reality with gentleness instead of frustration. It's the art of breathing deeply in the midst of uncertainty, knowing that peace is possible even when perfection isn't. When we accept what is, we make space for healing, clarity, and new beginnings.

As of this writing, I've been married for more than twenty-five years. Over time, I've learned that acceptance is one of the foundations of love. I often tell young women that when they're looking for a life partner, they must understand that they cannot change another person. The only person they can truly change is themselves.

Instead of hoping someone will become who you want them to be, look at their flaws and ask yourself, *Can I live with this for a lifetime?* If the answer is yes — if their imperfections are ones you can embrace or grow with — then the relationship is worth nurturing. But if those traits would lead to resentment or sadness, it may be kinder to let go and make space for something that aligns more peacefully with your heart. Once you accept the truth that the only change you can or should expect to make is within yourself, it helps to let go of the daily frustrations.

Using your kitchen timer, the timer on your stove, or an app on your phone, set your timer for five minutes.

Close your eyes and take a deep, cleansing breath.

Think about something in your life that feels out of your control. Is it a situation, person, or outcome?

As you inhale, silently repeat: *"My thoughts do not mean anything."*

As you exhale, whisper: *"I release this moment to peace."*

Notice how the mind quiets when you stop labeling your experience. In that stillness, you may sense something sacred — a softness, a calm presence that gently reminds you that everything is unfolding as it should.

When your timer ends, say, *"Thank you for the peace that comes from letting go and allowing life to simply be."*

Optional Journaling Exercise

Take a few quiet minutes to reflect on today's theme – Acceptance.

Ask yourself:

- What situation am I resisting right now, and why?

- What story or thought have I attached to it that keeps me from peace?

- How would it feel to view this situation without judgment and to simply let it be?

- What truths emerge when I remember that my thoughts are not facts, but choices?

Write freely without judgment. Let your thoughts flow naturally. When you're finished, close your journal, take a deep breath, and say, *"Thank you for giving me the ability to accept what I cannot change."*

36. Self-Worth

*"Our deepest fear is not that we are
inadequate. Our deepest fear is that we
are powerful beyond measure."*
Marianne Williamson

Many of us spend our lives doubting our worth. We believe we must earn love, success, or belonging through achievement or perfection. But true self-worth has nothing to do with accomplishment. It's the quiet understanding that you were born worthy, and nothing can add to or take away from that truth.

Marianne Williamson reminds us that what we truly fear isn't failure. It's our own light. We're afraid of how radiant, capable, and divine we actually are. We shrink ourselves to fit in, to stay safe, or to keep others comfortable. Yet the world doesn't need smaller versions of us; it needs our full, authentic selves... unafraid to shine.

A Course in Miracles teaches this same truth in *Lesson 62:* *"Forgiveness is my function as the light of the world."* It explains that when we recognize the light within ourselves, we naturally extend it to others. The course reminds us that we are creations of divine love, and therefore, our worth is inherent, not something to be earned or measured.

It also says, *"Your worth is established by God. Nothing you do or think or wish or make can establish it, or increase it, or lessen it."* (A Course in Miracles, Text I.VII.2:3–5)

This means that your self-worth is unshakable. It doesn't rise and fall with mistakes, opinions, or rejection. You are not what you've done, nor what's been done to you. You are, and have always been, enough.

When you embrace your light, you don't become arrogant. You become free. You begin to live from a place of quiet power, grace, and compassion.

Using your kitchen timer, the timer on your stove, or an app on your phone, set your timer for five minutes.

Close your eyes and place your hand over your heart.

Breathe deeply and imagine a warm light glowing in your chest. With each inhale, the light grows stronger.

With each exhale, it radiates outward.

Silently or verbally repeat: *"My worth is unchanging."*

If doubts or judgments arise, let them drift by without attachment. You don't need to fix or prove anything. Simply return to that light within you.

When your timer ends, say, *"Thank you for reminding me that I am enough and that my worth was never in question."*

Optional Journaling Exercise

Take a few quiet minutes to reflect on today's theme – Self-Worth.

Ask yourself:

- When have I forgotten my worth, and what helped me remember it?

- What does it feel like to stand in my own light without apology?

- How do I let the opinions of others shape how I see myself and how can I release that?

- What would change in my life if I fully believed I was already enough?

Write freely without judgment. Let your thoughts flow naturally. When you're finished, close your journal, take a deep breath, and say, *"I am worthy."*

_____

_____

_____

_____

_____

_____

_____

_____

_____

_____

37. *Perseverance*

*"I am not afraid of storms, for I am
learning how to sail my ship."*
Louisa May Alcott

Whenever I meet someone new and share pieces of my story such as delivering my first daughter stillborn and losing another baby, escaping three kidnapping attempts, being stalked and receiving death threats for years because of my wrongful conviction work, or caring for my disabled daughter who needed complete support for six years, they often respond with sympathy. They say things like, "I'm so sorry," or "How did you get through that?"

But to me, these experiences aren't tragedies that define me. They are chapters that shaped me. They are the winds and waves that taught me how to sail my ship. Each trial carved out a deeper understanding of who I am and what I'm capable of. If I hadn't faced loss, who would I be? If I hadn't relied on myself to escape danger, who would I be?

Perseverance isn't about pretending the sea is calm. It's about learning to navigate it with faith and courage when the storm won't stop. It's discovering that you are stronger than the waves that once threatened to drown you.

With each storm, we learn balance. We learn to trust our intuition, to keep moving forward even when visibility is low, and to believe that calmer waters lie ahead. Perseverance doesn't come from perfection. It comes from progress, from the quiet decision to rise one more time than we fall.

Using your kitchen timer, the timer on your stove, or an app on your phone, set your timer for five minutes.

Close your eyes and take a slow, steady breath in through your nose and out through your mouth.

Think about one storm you've weathered… a time when you weren't sure you'd make it through but somehow did. What kept you moving? Who or what helped you stay afloat?

As you breathe in, silently say, *"I am stronger than I knew."*

As you exhale, release any lingering fear from that time. Let it drift away like waves receding from shore.

When your timer ends, say, *"Thank you for every storm that taught me how to sail."*

Optional Journaling Exercise

Take a few quiet minutes to reflect on today's theme – Perseverance.

Ask yourself:

- What challenges in my life have taught me strength, patience, or resilience?

- How did I change after facing those storms mentally, emotionally, or spiritually?

- What helps me stay grounded when life feels uncertain or overwhelming?

- How can I use what I've learned from my struggles to help guide or comfort someone else?

Write freely without judgment. Let your thoughts flow naturally. When you're finished, close your journal, take a deep breath, and say, *"Thank you for allowing me to persevere."*

_____

_____

_____

_____

_____

_____

_____

_____

_____

_____

_____

_____

38. Freedom

*"The function of freedom is to free
someone else." Toni Morrison*

The idea of freedom comes in many forms. There are the physical limitations or restrictions that make us feel trapped, and there are the psychological ones — the burdens, stigmas, and expectations of others and of society. Then there are the limitations we quietly place on ourselves. The ones born from fear, low self-esteem, or the belief that we are not enough.

According to psychologists, freedom is not the absence of responsibility, but the ability to choose your response. True freedom comes from self-awareness, from recognizing the patterns and beliefs that keep us bound and choosing differently. We cannot always control our circumstances, but we can control how we think, how we act, and how we love through them.

Toni Morrison's words remind us that freedom is not meant to be hoarded. It's meant to be shared. When one woman finds her voice, she creates space for another to find hers. When we break a generational cycle or step out of silence, we make it easier for someone else to do the same.

Freedom expands when we live authentically, speak truthfully, and love fearlessly. It grows every time we say "no" to oppression, to self-doubt, and to anything that dims our light. And the most radical act of freedom begins within ourselves when we make the decision to no longer be held hostage by our past or by the opinions of others.

Using your kitchen timer, the timer on your stove, or an app on your phone, set your timer for five minutes.

Close your eyes and take a slow, deep breath.

Think about a time when you felt truly free. Perhaps it was speaking your truth, setting a boundary, or finally letting go of something that no longer served you.

As you breathe in, picture that freedom as a bright light expanding in your chest.

As you exhale, imagine that light reaching someone else who needs courage... a friend, a loved one, or even a stranger.

Each breath becomes an act of liberation. First for you, then for others. Imagine you're on a plane and put the oxygen mask on yourself first, then give oxygen to someone else.

When your timer ends, say, *"Thank you for the freedom to live as I am and the courage to help others do the same."*

Optional Journaling Exercise

Take a few quiet minutes to reflect on today's theme – Freedom.

Ask yourself:

- What does freedom mean to me emotionally, spiritually, or in my daily life?

- What fears, expectations, or limitations have I placed on myself that keep me from being fully free?

- Who in my life has helped me find my voice or encouraged me to live authentically?

- How can I use my freedom — my story, my strength, or my compassion — to help someone else find theirs?

Write freely without judgment. Let your thoughts flow naturally. When you're finished, close your journal, take a deep breath, and say, *"Thank you for my freedom."*

_____

_____

_____

_____

_____

_____

_____

_____

_____

_____

_____

_____

_____

_____

39. Healing

*"At the end of the day, we can endure
much more than we think we can."*
Frida Kahlo

Throughout history, the human race has endured unimaginable pain in wars, pandemics, famine, loss, and heartbreak. Yet we continue to rise. We rebuild cities after destruction, restore hope after despair, and find beauty again in the ashes of what was lost. This is the essence of the human spirit: our ability not only to survive, but to keep loving, creating, and believing even when we are wounded.

Since my daughter's diagnoses, I've learned that healing isn't always a return to what once was. People often tell her they hope or pray for her recovery, and while kind, those words can be difficult to hear, because she will never fully recover. We often forget that *normal* changes depending on our perspective.

Endurance itself — the quiet decision to keep going when nothing feels certain — becomes the new *normal*. Anyone who has experienced great loss understands this truth. Healing doesn't always mean restoration. Sometimes it means adaptation, courage, and learning to live gracefully with what remains.

The body may not always recover, the heart may always ache, but the soul learns how to carry both the pain and the light at once.

Frida Kahlo, who painted through relentless physical suffering, understood that healing is not the absence of pain but the transformation of it. She turned agony into art, showing that beauty can grow from brokenness and that endurance itself is a form of healing.

Human beings have always adapted in the face of loss. We evolve through grief and grow stronger through struggle. It is this capacity for endurance that has carried humanity forward generation after generation through wars, plagues, pandemics, oppression, and personal heartbreaks. Even when healing doesn't come in the way we expect, our strength allows us to move through the pain and find meaning within it.

Healing, then, is not a destination. It's a journey of remembrance... remembering that even when everything else is taken away, courage remains.

Using your kitchen timer, the timer on your stove, or an app on your phone, set your timer for five minutes.

Close your eyes and take a deep, steady breath.

Think of something you have survived. Was it a season of illness, grief, fear, or loss? Acknowledge how far you've come since then.

As you breathe in, imagine drawing strength from every person throughout history who has endured... from those who rebuilt their lives after loss, to those who loved again after heartbreak.

As you exhale, release the belief that healing must mean "going back" to who you once were. Instead, honor the new strength that has taken root in you.

Repeat silently or verbally: "I am healing, even when I am still hurting. My strength is my proof of life."

When your timer ends, place your hand over your heart and say, *"Thank you for the strength to endure, and for the light that still shines within me."*

Optional Journaling Exercise

Take a few quiet minutes to reflect on today's theme – Healing.

Ask yourself:

- What have I endured that once felt impossible to survive?

- How has pain reshaped me or revealed new strengths within me?

- What does healing mean to me — physically, emotionally, or spiritually?

- How can I honor my own endurance while giving myself grace for the parts still mending?

Write freely without judgment. Let your thoughts flow naturally. When you're finished, close your journal, take a deep breath, and say, *"Thank you for healing me."*

_____

_____

_____

_____

_____

40. Renewal

*"You cannot get through a single day
without having an impact on the world
around you. What you do makes a
difference, and you have to decide what
kind of difference you want to make."*
Jane Goodall

Renewal isn't about starting over. It's about returning to yourself. It's the quiet realization that even after the harshest winters, the ground still remembers how to bloom. Every day is a chance to begin again by making a small difference, forgiving, restoring hope, or simply choosing kindness over indifference.

Jane Goodall's words remind us that renewal is inseparable from responsibility. What we give to the world — our words, our choices, our compassion — becomes part of the greater cycle of life. Renewal is both inward and outward. It begins with healing ourselves and extends to the ways we care for others and for the earth.

Throughout history, humanity has rebuilt itself again and again after wars, after disasters, and after loss. And yet, renewal also happens in the unseen corners of everyday life when a heart learns to trust again, or a mother rediscovers joy after grief, or a stranger offers help with no expectation of return. These moments may seem small, but they ripple outward, shaping the world in unseen ways.

You don't need a grand gesture to renew your life. Sometimes it begins with a breath, a new thought, or a single act of kindness. Renewal is faith in motion. It's the belief that what is broken can still be made whole, that what has fallen asleep can awaken once more.

Using your kitchen timer, the timer on your stove, or an app on your phone, set your timer for five minutes.

Close your eyes and take a slow, intentional breath.

Picture a small green sprout breaking through the soil after a long winter. That sprout is your renewal. It's fragile, but full of life.

As you breathe in, imagine drawing in fresh energy, possibility, and purpose.

As you exhale, release the weight of yesterday. Let go of the expectations, guilt, and self-doubt that no longer serve you. Feel yourself rooted in this moment, connected to all living things.

Repeat silently or verbally: *"I am being renewed. My actions, however small, create ripples of light."*

When your timer ends, say, *"Thank you for the grace of new beginnings, and for the strength to make a difference."*

Optional Journaling Exercise

Take a few quiet minutes to reflect on today's theme – Renewal.

Ask yourself:

- What does renewal mean to me at this stage of my life?

- In what ways can I begin again in thought, action, or belief?

- How can I use my daily choices to create a positive impact on others or the world around me?

- What small act of renewal for myself or someone else can I offer today?

Write freely without judgment. Let your thoughts flow naturally. When you're finished, close your journal, take a deep breath, and say, *"Thank you for renewing me."*

_____

_____

_____

_____

_____

_____

_____

_____

_____

_____

_____

41. Strength of Spirit

"I am deliberate and afraid of nothing."

Audre Lorde

Strength of spirit isn't loud or boastful. It's quiet and unwavering, a flame that refuses to go out no matter how strong the wind blows. It's the will to keep standing when the ground beneath you shifts, to keep loving when the world feels cruel, and to keep believing that light still exists in the darkest places.

Audre Lorde's words are a declaration of power. Not dominance, but presence. To be deliberate is to live with intention, to choose your truth even when fear tells you otherwise. It's the courage to speak when silence feels safer and to move forward even when your voice shakes.

Throughout history, women have embodied this strength in ways that changed the world. Harriet Tubman guided souls to freedom under the cover of night. Malala Yousafzai stood up for education, even with attempts on her life. Countless unnamed women have held families, communities, and movements together with no more than sheer will and faith.

Strength of spirit is not about never breaking. It's about rising from the fracture with more wisdom and strength. It's resilience shaped by love, courage born from compassion, and power grounded in peace.

Every person carries that same flame within them. It lives in your heart each time you choose kindness over bitterness, truth over convenience, or hope over despair. When you act with intention, when you live deliberately, you strengthen not only your own spirit but the collective spirit of humanity.

Using your kitchen timer, the timer on your stove, or an app on your phone, set your timer for five minutes.

Close your eyes and take a deep, steady breath.

Think of a time when fear tried to silence you... when speaking up, standing firm, or being authentic felt risky, yet you did it anyway.

As you breathe in, imagine courage filling your lungs.

As you exhale, release the need for approval or safety that keeps your spirit small.

See yourself surrounded by light, the same flame that carried those before you who dared to live boldly and truthfully.

Repeat silently or verbally: *"I am deliberate. I am brave. My spirit cannot be broken."*

When your timer ends, say, *"Thank you for the strength to live with purpose and to meet life with an open, fearless heart."*

Optional Journaling Exercise

Take a few quiet minutes to reflect on today's theme – Strength of Spirit.

Ask yourself:

- What does living deliberately mean to me in this season of life?

- When have I felt fear, but chose to act from courage instead?

- Who inspires me to live with integrity, truth, and inner strength, and why?

- How can I nurture my spirit so that it remains strong, steady, and fearless even in uncertainty?

Write freely without judgment. Let your thoughts flow naturally. When you're finished, close your journal, take a deep breath, and say, *"Thank you for creating a strong spirit within me."*

_____

_____

_____

_____

_____

_____

_____

_____

_____

_____

_____

42. Recovery

"Hope begins in the dark, the stubborn hope that if you just show up and try to do the right thing, the dawn will come."
Anne Lamott

Recovery begins not in triumph, but in the shadows, in the quiet, unseen moments when you keep showing up, even when everything feels lost. Hope, as Anne Lamott reminds us, is not loud or certain. It's stubborn. It's the candle that refuses to go out, even when surrounded by darkness.

Throughout history, people have turned toward light in their hardest hours. Ancient sailors navigated by the stars, trusting what they could not yet see. Farmers planted seeds in barren soil, believing the earth would wake again. And healers across cultures taught that renewal requires surrender... the willingness to trust that what is broken will, in time, find its own way back to some new form of wholeness.

A Course in Miracles teaches a similar truth. In Lesson 75: *"The light has come,"* we're reminded that recovery isn't something we force. It's something we allow.

The course says:

"The light has come. I have forgiven the world."

This line reflects a sacred shift from fear to peace, from pain to acceptance. The "light" it speaks of is not external rescue, but the inner awareness that healing is possible the moment we stop resisting it. Forgiveness of ourselves, of others, of life for not being what we expected is the bridge between darkness and dawn.

Recovery, then, is an act of faith. It's showing up one small step at a time, even when the path ahead is dim. It's trusting that the same light that guided those before you still lives within you. And sometimes, recovery isn't about returning to who you were. It's about becoming someone stronger, softer, and more awake than you imagined you could be.

When the night feels long, remember that every dawn begins in darkness. Healing often comes disguised as endurance. And even when you can't see the light, it's still there waiting for you to turn toward it.

Using your kitchen timer, the timer on your stove, or an app on your phone, set your timer for five minutes.

Close your eyes and take a deep, slow breath. Feel your feet on the ground. It's solid, steady, and here.

Think of something in your life that you're still healing from... perhaps a loss, an illness, or a season of uncertainty.

As you breathe in, whisper softly: *"The light has come."*

As you exhale, imagine a faint sunrise in your heart. It will be dim at first but grow brighter with every breath.

Recovery rarely happens all at once. It unfolds like the first morning you smile again, the day you find yourself humming, or the moment you realize the pain doesn't consume you anymore.

Let yourself rest in that light. Not because the pain is gone, but because you've chosen to believe that peace is possible.

When your timer ends, say, *"Thank you for the courage to begin again, and for the light that never leaves, even in darkness."*

Optional Journaling Exercise

Take a few quiet minutes to reflect on today's theme – Recovery.

Ask yourself:

- What does recovery mean to me right now? Is it healing, acceptance, or rediscovery?

- What small signs of light have appeared in my life, even when I wasn't looking for them?

- How can I honor my progress, even if I'm still in the middle of my healing journey?

- What would it look like to trust that I'm already being guided toward peace?

Write freely without judgment. Let your thoughts flow naturally. When you're finished, close your journal, take a deep breath, and say, *"Thank you for the new day."*

_____

_____

_____

_____

43. Transformation

*"Nothing ever goes away until it has
taught us what we need to know."*
Pema Chödrön

Transformation is not a single moment of awakening. It's a process of being shaped by what we experience, sometimes painfully, sometimes beautifully. The lessons we resist most are often the ones that change us most deeply. Pema Chödrön reminds us that life repeats its teachings until we learn from them, not to punish us, but to guide us closer to wisdom.

Every person carries a story of becoming. We are sculpted by our heartbreaks, humbled by our failures, and softened by our losses. Growth doesn't mean avoiding pain. It means allowing it to teach us compassion, strength, and understanding.

Throughout history, humanity has evolved through transformation. Civilizations rebuilt after collapse, individuals found faith after despair, and families healed after generations of silence. Transformation, at its core, is the art of turning suffering into insight.

When you feel stuck or burdened by something that keeps resurfacing, whether it be a fear, a relationship pattern, or a wound that won't seem to heal, ask what it's trying to show you. There is always a message waiting within the discomfort.

Transformation doesn't demand perfection or constant positivity. It asks only for presence, for the willingness to stay awake to your own becoming. When you stop running from pain and start listening to it, you discover that what you thought was an ending is really an opening.

Using your kitchen timer, the timer on your stove, or an app on your phone, set your timer for five minutes.

Close your eyes and take a slow, deep breath.

Think of a situation or challenge in your life that keeps resurfacing. What is something you've wished would simply go away?

Instead of resisting it, imagine sitting beside it, listening.

Ask: *"What are you trying to teach me?"*

As you inhale, breathe in understanding and acceptance.

As you exhale, release judgment, impatience, and fear. Let your breath soften the hard edges of whatever lesson life is asking you to learn.

Transformation often happens not in the breakthrough moment, but in the small, steady choices to see differently, to forgive, and to remain open.

When your timer ends, say, *"Thank you for the lessons that shape me, and for the courage to become new."*

Optional Journaling Exercise

Take a few quiet minutes to reflect on today's theme – Transformation.

Ask yourself:

- What challenge in my life continues to repeat itself and what might it be trying to teach me?

- How have my past struggles transformed me into who I am today?

- What am I resisting that may actually be guiding me toward growth?

- How can I honor my transformation as an ongoing process, rather than a final destination?

Write freely without judgment. Let your thoughts flow naturally. When you're finished, close your journal, take a deep breath, and say, *"Thank you for transforming me."*

_____

_____

_____

_____

_____

_____

_____

_____

Phase 4: Abundance and Perspective

44. Gratitude

"'Thank you' is the best prayer that anyone could say. I say that one a lot. Thank you expresses extreme gratitude, humility, understanding." Alice Walker

When *The Color Purple* premiered at the theater where I worked as a teenager in the 1980s, it changed the way I saw the world. I was a white girl raised in an environment steeped in racial slurs and intolerance. Alice Walker's story opened a door I hadn't known existed. Until then, the only Black families I saw on television — in shows like *The Cosby Show* and *Good Times* — portrayed lives that felt not unlike my own. There were challenges, of course, but they were presented as part of the humor and heart of everyday life.

The Color Purple revealed something deeper.

Through Celie, Sophia, and every character who suffered because of their gender or the color of their skin, I was given a glimpse into another reality, one shaped by pain, strength, and grace.

Though I grew up poor and felt unloved, I recognized my privilege in ways I hadn't before. I couldn't know what it was like to live in their skin, but I understood what it felt like to be hated for something I couldn't change... to be the target of school bullies who mocked what nature gave to me, the bump

209

in my nose. That shared sense of pain, though born from different worlds, gave birth to true empathy.

My gratitude for Alice Walker and for all the brave authors and artists who share their truth has deepened through time. Their courage gave me perspective and the humility to understand that even in hardship, I was blessed. Gratitude became not just a feeling, but a way of seeing: a lens through which the world grew wider, kinder, and more connected.

One of the moments that touches me the most in *The Color Purple* is when Celie, who has endured a lifetime of cruelty and loss, finally finds her voice. She looks at the man who tormented her and says, "I may be poor, I may be black, I may even be ugly, but dear God, I'm here! I'm here!" That line has stayed with me ever since I first heard it, and I tear up every time I watch the movie. It's a declaration of gratitude in its purest form. Not for circumstance, but for existence itself.

Alice Walker taught us that gratitude isn't about pretending everything is perfect. It's about acknowledging that, despite pain or hardship, we still have the gift of presence. As Celie said, we are still here, still breathing, still capable of love, growth, and grace.

I challenge you to watch the movie if you haven't seen it. It remains my all-time favorite. And as you go about your day, carry a bit of Celie's strength and grace with you.

Using your kitchen timer, the timer on your stove, or an app on your phone, set your timer for five minutes.

Close your eyes and take a slow, steady breath.

Think about a story, movie, person, or experience that opened your eyes to a truth you hadn't seen before. What is something that shifted your understanding of yourself or others?

As you breathe in, imagine that awareness filling you with light.

As you exhale, whisper, *"Thank you."*

Let gratitude expand through you, not for perfection, but for perspective. For the lessons that made you softer, wiser, and more awake.

Gratitude is not blind optimism. It's the courage to look at life honestly and to see pain and beauty side by side and still choose appreciation. When we notice the small, sacred moments of grace hidden in our daily lives, whether it's a kind word, a sunrise, or a story that opens our hearts, we realize abundance has been here all along.

When your timer ends, say, *"Thank you for the gift of awareness, for the stories that teach me, and for the eyes to see abundance in all things."*

Optional Journaling Exercise

Take a few quiet minutes to reflect on today's theme – Gratitude.

Ask yourself:

- Who or what has helped me see life from a new perspective?

- How has empathy deepened my sense of gratitude and connection to others?

- What simple blessings or overlooked gifts bring richness to my daily life?

- How can I express gratitude not just in words, but in the way I live and see the world?

Write freely without judgment. Let your thoughts flow naturally. When you're finished, close your journal, take a deep breath, and say, *"Thank you."*

_____

_____

_____

_____

_____

_____

_____

_____

_____

_____

_____

_____

45. Abundance

"When you realize there is nothing lacking, the whole world belongs to you."
Lao Tzu

True abundance doesn't come from possessions, but from perception. It's the awareness that what we already have, such as breath, love, sunlight, and compassion, is enough. When we stop measuring life by what we acquire, we begin to see that we already live in the midst of plenty.

There's an ancient story told in many cultures about a fisherman and a businessman.

A wealthy businessman was vacationing in a small coastal village when he saw a fisherman pulling in his modest catch early one morning. Curious, the businessman asked why he didn't stay out longer and catch more fish.

The fisherman smiled and said, "I've caught enough to feed my family for the day."

"But what do you do with the rest of your time?" the businessman asked.

"I sleep late, play with my children, take a nap with my wife, and spend evenings with friends playing guitar and sharing laughter."

The businessman shook his head. "If you worked harder, you could buy a bigger boat, catch more fish, and eventually own a fleet! You could move to the city, build a company, and make a fortune."

"And then what?" the fisherman asked.

"Then," the businessman said proudly, "you could retire, move to a small village by the sea, sleep late, play with your children, take naps with your wife, and spend your evenings laughing with friends."

The fisherman smiled again, because he already had that.

This story reminds us that abundance isn't about having everything. It's about recognizing what's already enough. When we stop chasing what's next, we finally notice the richness of now.

For years, I worked as a ghostwriter and editor for a man who taught prosperity from a biblical perspective. One of his favorite lessons was to ask his students, "If I handed you a large sum of money right now, what would you do with it when you walk out of this room?" Some said they'd pay off debts, but others would buy a house, a car, or something they wanted. Then he smiled and asked, "What if you realized that your life is already full enough and that you don't need anything more to feel blessed?"

That question stayed with me. Like the fisherman in the story, I began to see abundance not as what I could earn, but as what I could appreciate. It shifted my focus from *getting* to *being*. From striving to noticing. From scarcity to gratitude.

Abundance is not accumulation; it's alignment. It's gratitude in motion. It's the moment you realize that joy doesn't come from adding more, but from appreciating what's here. The world belongs to those who see it through the eyes of enough.

Using your kitchen timer, the timer on your stove, or an app on your phone, set your timer for five minutes.

Close your eyes and take a slow, deep breath.

As you inhale, think about the many forms of wealth in your life — love, time, laughter, kindness, health, and wisdom.

As you exhale, release the illusion that abundance only comes from material things.

Picture yourself as the fisherman in the story. Allow yourself to feel content, fulfilled, and surrounded by what truly matters.

Breathe in gratitude for what you already have. Breathe out any sense of lack.

As you sit in stillness, repeat: *"I have enough. I am enough. My life is full."*

When your timer ends, say, *"Thank you for the abundance that fills my life, and for the eyes to recognize it."*

Optional Journaling Exercise

Take a few quiet minutes to reflect on today's theme – Abundance.

Ask yourself:

- What does abundance mean to me and how has that definition changed over time?

- When have I felt truly rich in spirit, even when I had little materially?

- What in my life today reminds me that I already have "enough"?

- How can I share my abundance, my time, compassion, wisdom, or love with others?

Write freely without judgment. Let your thoughts flow naturally. When you're finished, close your journal, take a deep breath, and say, *"Thank you for all I have."*

_____

_____

_____

_____

_____

_____

_____

_____

_____

_____

_____

_____

46. Prosperity

*"Prosperity is a flow of energy that
mirrors your state of gratitude."*
Deepak Chopra

As mentioned in the previous exercise, I once edited for a man who taught prosperity from both a practical and spiritual perspective. One of his core principles, and one I still carry with me today, is the idea of *flow*. When you live in the cycle of flow, everything you need moves to and through you without fear or desperation about where it comes from or when it will arrive.

In this state, prosperity stops being about accumulation and becomes about *alignment*. When your heart and intentions are aligned with gratitude, you create a current of energy that invites blessings into your life and allows them to move freely through it. You stop clinging to outcomes or possessions, and instead, you participate in the natural rhythm of giving and receiving.

Deepak Chopra calls prosperity an energy field, not a destination or a number, but a frequency we tune into through gratitude, generosity, and trust. When we cling tightly to control, we block that current. When we loosen our grip, acknowledge what we already have, and share from a place of love, life begins to flow again.

Flow is not passive; it's responsive. It's about taking inspired action without anxiety, and trusting that the right opportunities, people, and provisions will arrive at the right time. Prosperity comes from participation in that rhythm and knowing that every act of kindness, every prayer, every bit of gratitude adds to the cycle that sustains us all.

When we learn to live in flow, prosperity stops feeling like something to chase and starts feeling like something to *remember*. It's always been here, waiting for us to open our hands.

In *A Course in Miracles,* lesson 108, prosperity isn't measured by possessions or wealth, but by awareness of our divine connection. The Course teaches that *"To have, give all to all."* At first, that seems paradoxical, but it's a lesson about flow. It's the truth that what we give freely from love can never be lost.

When we give kindness, forgiveness, or compassion, those same energies return to us in multiplied form. Prosperity, then, is not accumulation but circulation. It's the movement of love, gratitude, and grace through our lives.

The Course reminds us that when we withhold love out of fear, we create a sense of lack; when we extend it, we experience abundance. In this way, giving becomes receiving, and gratitude becomes the channel through which prosperity flows.

Using your kitchen timer, the timer on your stove, or an app on your phone, set your timer for five minutes.

Close your eyes and take a slow, steady breath.

As you inhale, imagine drawing in light and it's the flow of abundance, opportunity, and peace.

As you exhale, release resistance, fear, and the need to control outcomes.

Picture yourself standing in a gentle stream with water moving around you. It's cool, constant, and effortless. This is prosperity: a flow that nourishes you and those around you. You don't need to chase the current. you only need to stay open to it.

Now, think of one area of your life where you've been trying too hard to force an outcome.

Ask yourself: What would happen if I trusted the flow instead?

Let your breath move with the rhythm of that flow, in and out, giving and receiving, trusting and releasing.

When your timer ends, say, *"Thank you for the flow of good that moves through me and for the peace that comes from trust."*

Optional Journaling Exercise

Take a few quiet minutes to reflect on today's theme – Prosperity.

Ask yourself:

- What does prosperity mean to me beyond money or material success?

- Where in my life do I feel "stuck," and how can I invite more flow into that area?

- What fears or beliefs keep me from trusting that I am provided for?

- How can I give time, love, kindness, or creativity in ways that keep the energy of abundance moving?

Write freely without judgment. Let your thoughts flow naturally. When you're finished, close your journal, take a deep breath, and say, *"Thank you for the flow of good in my life."*

_____

_____

_____

_____

_____

_____

_____

_____

_____

_____

_____

_____

_____

_____

47. Opportunity

"Option A is not available. Let's kick the hell out of Option B." Sheryl Sandberg

We've all heard the story about the man stranded in his home during a flood who prays for God to save him. As the water rises, a neighbor offers him a ride in a truck, then rescuers arrive in a boat, and finally, a helicopter hovers above. Each time, he waves them away, insisting that God will deliver him. When he drowns and meets God, he asks, "Why didn't you save me?"

God replies, "I sent you a truck, a boat, and a helicopter. What more did you expect?"

That story has always stayed with me because it reminds us that opportunity doesn't always look the way we imagine. Sometimes it comes disguised as hard work, detours, or even loss.

Sheryl Sandberg's words echo that truth. When life takes away Option A, it's not the end. It's an invitation to create something new with Option B.

Every challenge we face carries within it the seed of possibility. The key is awareness and the willingness to look around and recognize that the very thing we see as a setback might actually be the answer for which we've been waiting.

Gratitude opens that awareness. When we stop asking "Why me?" and start asking "What now?" we shift from waiting for rescue to partnering with life itself.

Opportunity often hides in the in-between, in closed doors, unexpected endings, or quiet moments when we least expect it. The more present we are, the more we notice the hands reaching out to help us or the doors opening.

Using your kitchen timer, the timer on your stove, or an app on your phone, set your timer for five minutes.

Close your eyes and take a deep, steady breath.

Think of a time in your life when something didn't go as planned, when a door closed, a path ended, or you experienced an outcome you couldn't control. Now, look a little closer. Was there another door that opened because of it? A new opportunity that only appeared once the first one was gone?

As you breathe in, invite awareness. Invite the ability to see clearly what's in front of you.

As you exhale, release frustration or regret for the way you thought things *should* have gone.

Life often answers our prayers in ways that don't match our expectations. But when we stay open, we begin to recognize that every detour can lead to something greater. Gratitude helps us notice those subtle moments of grace and say "yes" to what's next.

When your timer ends, say, *"Thank you for the doors I didn't expect, the lessons I didn't plan, and the opportunities that continue to find me."*

Optional Journaling Exercise

Take a few quiet minutes to reflect on today's theme – Opportunity.

Ask yourself:

- What opportunity in my life once looked like a disappointment or detour?

- How can I practice recognizing open doors, even when they look unfamiliar or uncomfortable?

- What role does gratitude play in helping me notice new possibilities?

- How can I act on the opportunities already in front of me today?

Write freely without judgment. Let your thoughts flow naturally. When you're finished, close your journal, take a deep breath, and say, *"Thank you for opportunities."*

_____

_____

_____

_____

_____

_____

_____

48. Growth

"Spiritual growth involves giving up the stories of your past so the universe can write a new one." Marianne Williamson

When you grow up being told you're not enough, or when you survive an abusive relationship that erodes your self-worth, it's easy to start believing the story your abuser wrote for you. When a teacher or friend says you'll never be good at ... fill in the blank... you believe them. You wear their words like truth until one day when you realize the story never belonged to you.

Growth begins in that moment of awareness. It's the quiet, powerful act of reclaiming your narrative, of deciding that your past may have shaped you, but it will not define you. As Marianne Williamson reminds us, spiritual growth asks us to release those old stories so that something new can take root.

There's an old story from the East about a monk who carried a heavy bag of stones up a mountain. When asked why, he said each stone represented an old wound or a resentment. When he finally reached the top, exhausted and trembling, he sat down and emptied the bag, one stone at a time. The mountain didn't change. His path didn't change. What changed was *him*. After releasing the burdens of his resentments and wounds, he was free to walk back down lighter and unburdened by what no longer served him.

Growth often looks like this. It's releasing, not adding. It's not about striving for more but learning to travel with less weight.

In *A Course in Miracles*, Lesson 132 teaches: "I loose the world from all I thought it was, and choose my own reality instead."

The Course reminds us that true growth is an undoing. It's a gentle unwinding of false beliefs we've inherited or internalized. It's an invitation to see the world, and ourselves, through love instead of fear. When we release the stories that kept us small, we allow the divine to rewrite the truth: that we are whole, worthy, and free.

Letting go doesn't mean forgetting or denying what happened; it means recognizing that you are no longer the person who needed to survive that version of your life. As I've expressed many times in these exercises, growth is not about perfection. It's about evolution. It's the willingness to outgrow the lies you were told and the limitations you once accepted. They don't define you.

When you surrender the old story, you make space for healing, purpose, and grace to move through you. The universe always meets us in that space, not to erase pain, but to transform it into wisdom.

Using your kitchen timer, the timer on your stove, or an app on your phone, set your timer for five minutes.

Close your eyes and take a slow, deep breath.

Think of one old story you've carried... a belief, memory, or label that no longer serves who you are becoming.

As you inhale, picture yourself gathering that story gently in your hands.

As you exhale, imagine placing it in the river of time, watching it drift away with gratitude for what it taught you.

Now, breathe into the space that story once occupied.

Feel the lightness. The openness. The possibility. Whisper to yourself: *"I release what was. I welcome what is yet to come."*

As the monk in the ancient story discovered, growth doesn't come from carrying more, but from setting down what no longer needs to be held. When your timer ends, say, *"Thank you for the courage to let go, and for the grace to grow."*

Optional Journaling Exercise

Take a few quiet minutes to reflect on today's theme – Growth.

Ask yourself:

- What story or belief about myself am I ready to release?

- How has holding onto that story protected me and how has it limited me?

- What truth would I like the universe to write for me now?

- How can I practice growth through gentleness rather than striving?

Write freely without judgment. Let your thoughts flow naturally. When you're finished, close your journal, take a deep breath, and say, *"Thank you for showing me that letting go allows me to grow."*

49. Lessons Learned

*"Character cannot be developed in ease
and quiet. Only through experience of
trial and suffering can the soul be
strengthened, ambition inspired, and
success achieved." Helen Keller*

One of the most poignant lessons I've learned in life is that not everyone will love me, or even like me, and that's okay. For a long time, I tried to shape myself into someone others would accept, smoothing out the edges of who I was so I could fit neatly into places I didn't belong. It took years, and more than a few heartbreaks, to understand that being true to myself would never require universal approval.

Some lessons arrive as sprinkles, others as storms. The hardest ones rarely come wrapped in comfort, yet they are the ones that shape us most. Life's difficulties teach us not just endurance, but discernment... the ability to recognize who we are, what we value, and what we will no longer tolerate.

Helen Keller's words remind us that character isn't built in ease, but in the friction of experience. Trial and suffering refine us. They strip away illusion and strengthen the spirit. When we face disappointment or rejection, it doesn't mean we've failed. It means we're being invited to grow in self-respect, compassion, and faith.

Over time, I've learned that every difficult moment carries a message: love yourself enough to keep walking, even when the path feels lonely. The people meant for you will meet you along the way, drawn not to your perfection, but to your truth.

Using your kitchen timer, the timer on your stove, or an app on your phone, set your timer for five minutes.

Close your eyes and take a slow, deep breath.

Think of one lesson that life taught you the hard way. Think of a moment that once felt painful, unfair, or confusing. Now, with the perspective of time, ask yourself: *What did I gain that I couldn't have learned any other way?*

As you inhale, breathe in acceptance for the person you were then and doing your best with what you knew.

As you exhale, breathe out forgiveness for yourself, for others, and for the experience itself.

Growth rarely comes wrapped in comfort. Sometimes it arrives through heartbreak, rejection, or disappointment. But within every difficult moment is a quiet invitation to return to yourself wiser, stronger, and more compassionate than before.

When your timer ends, say, *"Thank you for the lessons that shaped me, for the strength they awakened, and for the peace I've found in understanding."*

Optional Journaling Exercise

Take a few quiet minutes to reflect on today's theme – Lessons Learned.

Ask yourself:

- What difficult experience has taught me the most about who I am?

- How has rejection or loss shaped my ability to love and accept myself?

- What lesson in my life keeps repeating and what might it be trying to teach me?

- How can I turn my past wounds into wisdom that helps others?

Write freely without judgment. Let your thoughts flow naturally. When you're finished, close your journal, take a deep breath, and say, *"Thank you for the lessons of life."*

_____

_____

_____

_____

_____

_____

_____

_____

_____

_____

50. Change

"Seek not to change the world, but choose to change your mind about the world." A Course in Miracles

Change is inevitable, but transformation is a choice. We often try to control what happens around us — people, circumstances, even the future — believing that peace will come once everything falls into place. But *A Course in Miracles* reminds us that true change doesn't begin outside of us. It begins within.

When we change our perception, the world itself looks different. The same situation that once felt unbearable can become a lesson in patience. The same person who once seemed cruel can become a teacher of boundaries and self-worth. Change your mind, and what you see shifts in response.

There's an ancient parable that mirrors this idea. Two monks were walking through a village when they encountered a woman who needed help crossing a muddy road. One monk carried her across on his back and set her down safely on the other side. Hours later, the other monk said, "I can't believe you carried that woman. We're forbidden to touch them." The first monk smiled gently and replied, "I put her down hours ago. Why are you still carrying her?"

The story reminds us that real change isn't about the world or other people. It's about what we choose to carry in our minds and hearts. Sometimes, the greatest change is letting go.

Change is rarely comfortable. It can feel like loss, uncertainty, or even chaos. But every time we shift our perception from fear to love, we invite peace back into our lives. The world itself may not change overnight, but our experience of it transforms completely.

When you stop trying to change the world and instead allow it to teach you, life becomes less of a struggle and more of a partnership with grace.

Using your kitchen timer, the timer on your stove, or an app on your phone, set your timer for five minutes.

Close your eyes and take a slow, steady breath.

Think of something in your life that you've been trying to change such as a person, situation, or circumstance.

As you inhale, silently say: *"I am willing to see this differently."*

As you exhale, release the need to control how it changes.

Allow yourself to imagine what peace might feel like if you accepted this moment exactly as it is. Acceptance isn't giving up. It's making room for understanding. When you change how you look at something, you see what was always true beneath the surface.

When your timer ends, say, *"Thank you for the power to change my mind, and for the peace that comes from seeing with love."*

Optional Journaling Exercise

Take a few quiet minutes to reflect on today's theme – Change.

Ask yourself:

- What situation or person in my life am I trying to change right now?

- What would happen if I focused instead on changing how I *see* it?

- How has shifting my perception in the past brought unexpected peace or clarity?

- What fear or belief can I release today to allow true change to begin within me?

Write freely without judgment. Let your thoughts flow naturally. When you're finished, close your journal, take a deep breath, and say, *"Thank you for giving me the insight to change."*

_____

_____

_____

_____

_____

_____

_____

_____

_____

Final Thoughts

You've reached the final page of this journey which included fifty moments of reflection, awareness, and gratitude. Whether you completed each exercise daily, weekly, or whenever your heart called for stillness, you've done something extraordinary: you've shown up for yourself.

Gratitude is not a one-time practice. It's a way of seeing. Every breath, every challenge, every act of kindness is part of the unfolding miracle that is your life. By slowing down and giving these moments your attention, you've opened a doorway to peace, not because your circumstances changed, but because *you* changed.

There will always be more to learn, more to release, more to love. Growth doesn't end here. It continues with every act of noticing, every pause between thoughts, every "thank you" said to no one in particular.

As you move beyond these pages, carry with you the spirit of what you've practiced: patience when life feels uncertain, compassion when the world feels heavy, and gratitude as your compass through it all.

The extra pages that follow are yours to fill with reflections, prayers, dreams, or small moments of light. Use them freely. Let your handwriting become the continuation of this journey.

And whenever you lose your way, return to gratitude. It will always lead you home.

Thank you for walking this path. May your days be filled with peace, awareness, and love.

Watch for the second book, "More Five-Minute Gratitude" coming in 2026.

_____

_____

_____

_____

_____

_____

_____

_____

_____

_____

_____

_____

www.ingramcontent.com/pod-product-compliance
Lightning Source LLC
Chambersburg PA
CBHW051300120626
46547CB00015B/2027